Bliss
A Treasure-Trove of Smilies

Bliss
A Treasure-Trove of Smilies

Compiled by

Sharad Gupta

ALLIED PUBLISHERS PVT. LTD.

New Delhi • Mumbai • Kolkata • Lucknow • Chennai
Nagpur • Bangalore • Hyderabad • Ahmedabad

ALLIED PUBLISHERS PRIVATE LIMITED

1/13-14 Asaf Ali Road, **New Delhi**–110002
Ph.: 011-23239001 • E-mail: delhi.books@alliedpublishers.com

47/9 Prag Narain Road, Near Kalyan Bhawan, **Lucknow**–226001
Ph.: 0522-2209942 • E-mail: lko.books@alliedpublishers.com

17 Chittaranjan Avenue, **Kolkata**–700072
Ph.: 033-22129618 • E-mail: cal.books@alliedpublishers.com

15 J.N. Heredia Marg, Ballard Estate, **Mumbai**—400001
Ph.: 022-42126969 • E-mail: mumbai.books@alliedpublishers.com

60 Shiv Sunder Apartments (Ground Floor), Central Bazar Road,
Bajaj Nagar, **Nagpur**–440010
Ph.: 0712-2234210 • E-mail: ngp.books@alliedpublishers.com

F-1 Sun House (First Floor), C.G. Road, Navrangpura,
Ellisbridge P.O., **Ahmedabad**–380006
Ph.: 079-26465916 • E-mail: ahmbd.books@alliedpublishers.com

751 Anna Salai, **Chennai**–600002
Ph.: 044-28523938 • E-mail: chennai.books@alliedpublishers.com

5th Main Road, Gandhinagar, **Bangalore**–560009
Ph.: 080-22262081 • E-mail: bngl.books@alliedpublishers.com

3-2-844/6 & 7 Kachiguda Station Road, **Hyderabad**–500027
Ph.: 040-24619079 • E-mail: hyd.books@alliedpublishers.com

Website: www.alliedpublishers.com

© 2013, Sharad Gupta

ISBN: 978-81-8424-811-1

Published by Sunil Sachdev and printed by Ravi Sachdev at Allied Publishers Pvt. Ltd. (Printing Division), A-104 Mayapuri Phase II, New Delhi-110064

Preface

Human body is made of bones and flesh, but human mind is made of thoughts. We create our world by our thoughts, and thus we make our own heaven and our own hell. The happiness of our life depends on the quality of our thoughts.

Words that enlighten the soul are more precious than jewels. Words have the power to alter a person's thinking. Like a bee which keeps collecting honey from the blooming flowers, I began to collect such thoughts from whatever source I could lay my hands upon. This book is a collection of such thoughts.

These thoughts and essays provide perspective, inspiration and solace to stir echoes, to touch perceptions and ideas that might otherwise have remained idle and forgotten in the back of the mind. Like short fiction, each piece leads to a point of illumination, evoking an original, unmeditated response that we are sure to treasure.

We thankfully acknowledge the collection of these thoughts and articles from various sources, most of whom have given permission to edit and reproduce. Some could not be contacted but we could not resist the temptation to include their profound thoughts in this book, as we are sure of their implicit and gracious permission. Names of the authors of individual articles have not been mentioned as most of these are collective thoughts. These articles were collected in bits and pieces and names of some of the authors could not be traced. Anyway, the contributors are too magnanimous to mind such trivialities.

If these thoughts are able to provide you even a little joy, a little greater self-confidence, a little greater purity in life, I will consider my efforts greatly rewarded. Let these thoughts serve you as a change agent and provide you with a sense of fulfillment.

Take time to be friendly—it is the road to happiness;

Take time to love and to be loved—it is the privilege of Gods;

Take time to laugh—it is the music of the soul.

Life may not be the party we hoped for,

but while we are here we might as well dance.

* * *

A man asked, "I want happiness".

Lord Buddha said, first remove "I" that is ego.

Then remove "WANT" that is desire.

So now you are left with only "HAPPINESS".

Contents

Preface .... *v*

1. As High as You Can 1
2. Hot Chocolate 3
3. How to Stay Young 5
4. Letter from GOD 6
5. Life is Like Money 9
6. Perception 10
7. Solution to a Problem 12
8. Team Work 14
9. God and the Spider 16
10. Attitude 18
11. Coffee Beans 19
12. Should You be Reacting or Responding 21
   to a Situation?
13. Take off Your Blindfold 23
14. Proper Resource Utilization 24
15. God does not Exist 26
16. The Aging Phenomena 28
17. The Art of Giving 30
18. Why Women are so Special 32
19. The Cab Ride 34
20. The Savings Account 37
21. The Test of Three 39
22. Weakness or Strength 41
23. Wealth, Success and Love 43
24. What do You do all Day? 45
25. The Important Things in Life 47
26. A to Z of Life 49
27. The Pencil Story 53
28. Miracle 55

29. Never Judge Anyone by their Appearance 57
30. Until Death do Us Apart 59
31. Merry Christmas! 63
32. The Law of the Seed 68
33. Are You Good Enough? 69
34. What Happens in Heaven 70
35. The Law of the Garbage Truck 72
36. A Glass of Milk 73
37. Put the Glass Down Today! 75
38. This too will Pass 77
39. Love and Life 79
40. Building a Life 82
41. God's Clinic 83
42. Have Faith 84
43. I Wish You Enough 88
44. A Different Perspective 90
45. Something for God to Do 91
46. Priya and Her Mother-in-Law 93
47. The Pretty Lady 95
48. Burnt Toast 96
49. Heaven and Hell 97
50. Game of Potato 98
51. One Bedroom Flat 99
52. The Daffodil Principle 102
53. It is Easier to Criticize 105
54. A Dozen Questions to Ask Yourself 107
55. A Love Story of all Times 108
56. As You Sow, so shall You Reap 110
57. Make Room 115
58. The Missing Watch 116
59. Lessons of Life 117
60. Deposit 118
61. A Lizard Story 120

As High as You Can

Enough is Enough – I said.

One day I decided to quit...

I quit my job, my relationship, my spirituality...

I wanted to quit my life.

I went to the woods to have one last talk with God.

"God", I said. "Can you give me one good reason not to quit?"

His answer surprised me...

"Look around", He said. "Do you see the fern and the bamboo?"

"Yes", I replied.

"When I planted the fern and the bamboo seeds, I took very good care of them. I gave them light. I gave them water. The fern quickly grew from the earth. Its brilliant green covered the floor. Yet nothing came from the bamboo seed. But I did not quit on the bamboo."

"In the second year the fern grew more vibrant and plentiful. And again, nothing came from the bamboo seed. But I did not quit on the bamboo."

"In the third year there was still nothing from the bamboo seed. But I would not quit."

"In the fourth year, again, there was nothing from the bamboo seed. I would not quit."

"Then in the fifth year a tiny sprout emerged from the earth. Compared to the fern it was seemingly small and insignificant... But just 6 months later the bamboo rose to over 100 feet tall."

"It had spent five years growing roots."

"Those roots made it strong and gave it what it needed to survive."

"I would not give any of my creations a challenge it could not handle."

He said to me. "Did you know, my child, that all this time you have been struggling, you have actually been growing roots?"

"I would not quit on the bamboo. I will never quit on you."

"Don't compare yourself to others." He said.

"The bamboo had a different purpose than the fern. Yet they both make the forest beautiful."

"Your time will come", God said to me. "You will rise high."

"How high should I rise?" I asked.

"How high will the bamboo rise?" He asked in return.

"As high as it can." I answered.

"Yes." He said, "Give me glory by rising as high as you can."

If an egg is broken by an outside force ... a life ends.

If an egg breaks from within ... life begins.

Great things always begin from within.

Hot Chocolate

A group of graduates, well established in their careers, were talking at a reunion and decided to visit their old university professor.

During their visit, the conversation turned to complaints about stress in their work and lives.

Offering his guests hot chocolate, the professor went into the kitchen and returned with a large pot of hot chocolate and an assortment of cups—porcelain, glass, crystal, some plain looking, some expensive, some exquisite—telling them to help themselves to the hot chocolate.

When they all had a cup of hot chocolate in hand, the professor said: Notice that all the nice looking, expensive cups were taken, leaving behind the plain and cheap ones. While it is normal for you to want only the best for yourselves, that is the source of your problems and stress.

The cup that you're drinking from adds nothing to the quality of the hot chocolate. In most cases it is just more expensive and in some cases even hides what we drink.

What all of you really wanted was hot chocolate, not the cup; but you consciously went for the best cups. And then you began eyeing each other's cups.

Now consider this: Life is the hot chocolate; your job, money and position in society are the cups.

They are just tools to hold and contain life.

The cup you have does not define, nor change the quality of life you have.

Sometimes, by concentrating only on the cup, we fail to enjoy the hot chocolate God has provided us. God makes the hot chocolate, man chooses the cups. The happiest people don't have the best of everything. They just make the best of everything that they have.

Live simply.
Love generously.
Care deeply.
Speak kindly.
And enjoy your hot chocolate.

The most selfish 1 letter word is **I**, *Avoid it.*

The most satisfying 2-letter word is **WE**, *Trust it.*

The most poisonous 3-letter word is **EGO**, *Kill it.*

The most used 4-letter word is **LOVE**, *Value it.*

The most pleasing 5-letter word is **SMILE**, *Keep it.*

The fastest spreading 6-letter word is **RUMOUR**, *Ignore it.*

The hardest working 7-letter word is **SUCCESS**, *Achieve it.*

The most enviable 8-letter word is **JEALOUSY**, *Distance it.*

The most powerful 9-letter word is **KNOWLEDGE**, *Acquire it.*

The most essential 10-letter word is **CONFIDENCE**, *Use it.*

How to Stay Young

1. Throw out nonessential numbers. This includes age, weight and height. Let the doctor worry about them. That is why you pay him/her.

2. Keep cheerful friends. The grouches pull you down.

3. Keep learning. Learn more about computer, gardening, whatever. Never let the brain idle. An idle mind is the devil's workshop. And the devil's name is Alzheimer's.

4. Enjoy simple things. Laught often, long and loud. Laught until you gasp for breath.

5. The tears happen. Endure, grieve, and move on. The only person who is with us our entire life, is ourselves. Be ALIVE while you are alive.

6. Surround yourself with what you love, whether it's family, pets, music, plants, hobbies, whatever. Your home is your refuge.

7. Cherish your health. If it is good, preserve it. If it is unstable, improve it. If it is beyond what you can improve, get help.

8. Don't take guilt trips. Take a trip to the mall, to a city, to a foreign country, but not to where the guilt is.

9. Tell the people you love that you love them, at every opportunity. Spend some time with your loved ones, because they are not going to be around forever. Give a warm hug to them, because that is the only treasure you can give with your heart and it costs nothing.

10. Give time to love, give time to speak, and give time to share the precious thoughts in your mind.

Letter from GOD

My Dear Children (and believe me, that's all of you), I consider myself a pretty patient guy. I've been patient through your fashions, civilizations, wars and schemes, and the countless ways you take me for granted until you get yourselves into big trouble again and again. I want to let you know about some of the things that you do are starting to tick me off.

First of all, your religious rivalries are driving me up the wall. Let's get one thing straight. These are your religions, not mine. I'm beyond them all. Every one of your religions claims there is only one of Me (which by the way, is absolutely true). But in the very next breath, each religion claims that its holy book was written personally by me. Okay, listen up now, I'm your Father and Mother, and I don't play favourites among my children. Also, I hate to break it to you, but I don't write. My longhand is awful, and I've always been more of a 'doer' anyway. So all of your books were written by men and women. They were remarkable people, but they also made mistakes here and there. I made sure of that, so that you would never trust a written word more than your own living heart.

You act like I need you and your religions. Please, don't do me any favours. I can stand quite well on my own, thank you. I don't need you to defend me, and I don't need constant credit, I just want you to be good to each other.

And another thing, I don't get all worked up over money or politics, so stop dragging my name into your schemes. The thing is, I want you to stop thinking of religion as some sort of loyalty pledged to me. The true purpose of your religion is so that you can become more aware of me, not the other way round.

Believe Me, I know you already. I know what's in each of your hearts, and I love you with no strings attached. Lighten up and enjoy Me. That's what religion is best for. What you seem to forget is how mysterious I am.

You look at the petty differences in your scriptures and say, 'Well, if this is the truth, then that can't be! But instead of trying to figure out my paradoxes and unfathomable nature, which by the way, you never will, why not open your hearts to the simple common threads in all religions.

You know what I'm talking about. Love and respect everyone. Be kind, even when life is scary or confusing, take courage and be of good cheer, for I am always with you. Learn how to be quiet, so you can hear my still, soft voice (I don't like to shout). Hold back nothing from life, for the parts of you that can die surely will, and the parts that can't, won't. So don't worry, be happy.

Simple stuff. Why do you keep making it so complicated? It's like you're always looking for an excuse to be upset. And I'm very tired of being your main excuse. Do you think I care what you call me? Do you think I care which of my children you feel closest to?

You can call me and my children any name you choose, if only you would go about my business of loving one another as I love you. How can you keep neglecting something so simple? I'm not telling you to abandon your religions. Enjoy your religions, honor them, learn from them, and learn from your parents. But do you walk around telling everyone that your parents are better than theirs?

Each religion is unique for a reason. Each has a unique style so that people can find the best path for themselves.

If you really want to help them, commit yourselves to figuring out how to feed your hungry, clothe your naked, protect your abused, and shelter your poor. And just as importantly, make your own everyday life a shining example of good humour.

I'm not really ticked off. I just wanted to grab your attention because I hate to see your suffer. I want you to be happy.

Your One and Only

God

Always remember to forget
the things that made you sad,
But never forget to remember
the things that made you glad.

Always remember to forget
the friends that proved untrue,
But never forget to remember
those that have stuck by you.

Always remember to forget
the troubles that passed away
But never forget to remember
the blessings that come each day.

Life is Like Money

A well-known speaker started off his seminar by holding up a ₹ 1000 note. In the room of 200, he asked, "Who would like to have this ₹ 1000 note?"

Hands started going up.

He said, "I am going to give this ₹ 1000 to one of you but first, let me do this." He proceeded to crumple up the note.

He then asked, "Who still wants it?"

Still the hands were up in the air. "Well", he replied, "What if I do this?" And he dropped it on the ground and started to grind it into the floor with his shoe.

He picked it up, now crumpled and dirty. "Now, who still wants it?"

Still the hands went into the air.

"My friends, we have all learned a very valuable lesson. No matter what I did to the money, you still wanted it because it did not decrease in value. It was still worth ₹ 1000 note. Many times in our lives, we are dropped, crumpled, and grounded into the dirt by the decisions we make and the circumstances that come our way. We feel as though we are worthless. But no matter what has happened or what will happen, you will never lose your value."

Dirty or clean, crumpled or finely creased, you are still priceless to those who love you. The worth of our lives comes not in what we do or who we know, but by who we are. You are special—don't ever forget it.

Perception

In Washington DC, at a Metro Station, on a cold January morning in 2007, this man with a violin played six Bach pieces for about 45 minutes. During that time, approximately 2,000 people went through the station, most of them on their way to work. After about 3 minutes, a middle-aged man noticed that there was a musician playing. He slowed his pace and stopped for a few seconds, and then he hurried on to meet his schedule.

About 4 minutes later:

The violinist received his first dollar. A woman threw money in the hat and, without stopping, continued to walk.

At 6 minutes:

A young man leaned against the wall to listen to him, then looked at his watch and started to walk again.

At 10 minutes:

A 3-year old boy stopped, but his mother tugged him along hurriedly. The kid stopped to look at the violinist again, but the mother pushed hard and the child continued to walk, turning his head the whole time. This action was repeated by several other children, but every parent—without exception—forced their children to move on quickly.

At 45 minutes:

The musician played continuously. Only 6 people stopped and listened for a short while. About 20 gave money but continued to walk at their normal pace. The man collected a total of $32.

After 1 hour:

He finished playing and silence took over. No one noticed and no one applauded. There was no recognition at all.

No one knew this, but the violinist was Joshua Bell, one of the greatest musicians in the world. He played one of the most intricate pieces ever written, with a Stradivarius violin worth $3.5 million dollars. Two days before, Joshua Bell sold-out a theater in Boston where the seats averaged $100 each to sit and listen to him play the same music.

This is a true story. Joshua Bell, playing incognito in the DC Metro Station, was organized by the Washington Post as part of a social experiment about perception, taste and people's priorities.

This experiment raised several questions:

- In a common-place environment, at an inappropriate hour, do we perceive beauty?

- If so, do we stop to appreciate it?

- Do we recognise talent in an unexpected context?

One possible conclusion reached from this experiment could be this:

If we do not have a moment to stop and listen to one of the best musicians in the world, playing some of the finest music ever written, with one of the most beautiful instruments ever made...

How many other things are we missing as we rush through life?

Solution to a Problem

Many years ago, in a small village, a farmer had the misfortune of owing a large sum of money to a village moneylender. The moneylender, who was old and ugly, fancied the farmer's beautiful daughter. So he proposed a bargain. He said he would forego the farmer's debt if he could marry his daughter. Both the farmer and his daughter were horrified by the proposal.

So the cunning money-lender suggested that they let luck decide the matter. He told them that he would put a black pebble and a white pebble into an empty money bag. Then the girl would have to pick one pebble from the bag.

1. If she picked the black pebble, she would become his wife and her father's debt would be forgiven.

2. If she picked the white pebble she need not marry him and her father's debt would still be forgiven.

3. But if she refused to pick a pebble, her father would be thrown into jail.

They were standing on a pebble strewn path in the farmer's field. As they talked, the moneylender bent over to pick up two pebbles. As he picked them up, the sharp-eyed girl noticed that he had picked up two black pebbles and put them into the bag.

He then asked the girl to pick a pebble from the bag. Now, imagine that you were standing in the field. What would you have done if you were the girl? If you had to advice her, what would you have told her?

Careful analysis would produce three possibilities:

1. The girl should refuse to take a pebble.
2. The girl should show that there were two black pebbles in the bag and expose the money-lender as a cheat.
3. The girl should pick a black pebble and sacrifice herself in order to save her father from his debt and imprisonment.

Take a moment to ponder over the story. The above story is used with the hope that it will make us appreciate the difference between lateral and logical thinking. The girl's dilemma cannot be solved with traditional logical thinking. Think of the consequences if she chooses the above logical answers.

What would you recommend the girl to do?

Well, here is what she did...

The girl put her hand into the moneybag and drew out a pebble. Without Looking at it, she fumbled and let it fall onto the pebble-strewn path where it immediately became lost among all the other pebbles.

"Oh, how clumsy of me," she said. "But never mind, if you look into the bag for the one that is left, you will be able to tell which pebble I picked."

Since the remaining pebble is black, it must be assumed that she had picked the white one. And since the money-lender dared not admit his dishonesty, the girl changed what seemed an impossible situation into an extremely advantageous one.

Moral: Most complex problems do have a solution. What is needed is to rise one step higher to solve them.

Team Work

It was a sports stadium.

Eight Children were standing on the track to participate in a running event.

* Ready! * Steady! * Bang!!!

With the sound of toy pistol, all eight girls started running. Hardly had they covered ten to fifteen steps, when one of the smaller girls slipped and fell down. Due to bruises and pain, she started crying.

When the other seven girls heard the little girl cry, they stopped running, stood for a while and turned back.

Seeing the girl on the track they all ran to help. One among them bent down, picked her up and kissed her gently and enquired as to how she was. They then lifted the fallen girl, pacifying her.

Two of them held her firmly while all seven joined hands together and walked together towards the winning post.

There was pin drop silence at the spectator's stand.

Officials were shocked.

Slow claps multiplied to thousands as the spectators stood up in appreciation. Many eyes were filled with tears

YES. This happened in Hyderabad recently!

The sport was conducted by National Institute of Mental Health.

All these special girls had come to participate in this event. They were spastic children.

Yes, they were Mentally Challenged.

What did they teach the world?

- Teamwork.

- Humanity.

- Equality among all.

We can't do this ever because we have brains!

There is an Indian proverb or axiom that says that everyone is a house with four rooms:

- *physical*

- *mental*

- *emotional, and*

- *spiritual.*

Most of us tend to live in one room most of the time, but unless we go into every room every day, even if only to keep it aired, we are not a complete person.

God and the Spider

During World War II, a US marine was separated from his unit on a Pacific island. The fighting had been intense, and in the smoke and the crossfire he had lost touch with his comrades.

Alone in the jungle, he could hear enemy soldiers coming in his direction. Scrambling for cover, he found his way up a high ridge to several small caves in the rock. Quickly he crawled inside one of the caves. Although safe for the moment, he realized that once the enemy soldiers looking for him swept up the ridge, they would quickly search all the caves and he would be killed.

As he waited, he prayed, Lord, if it be your will, please protect me. Whatever your will though, I love you and trust you. Amen.

After praying, he lay quietly listening to the enemy begin to draw close. He thought, well, I guess the Lord isn't going to help me out of this one.

Then he saw a spider begin to build a web over the front of his cave. As he watched, listening to the enemy searching for him all the while, the spider layered strand after strand of web across the opening of the cave. Hah, he thought. What I need is a brick wall and what the Lord has sent me is a spider web. God does have a sense of humor.

As the enemy drew closer he watched from the darkness of his hideout and could see them searching one cave after another. As they came to his, he got ready to make his last stand. To his amazement, however, after glancing in the

16

direction of his cave, they moved on. Suddenly, he realized that with the spider web over the entrance, his cave looked as if no one had entered for quite a while. Lord, forgive me, prayed the young man. I had forgotten that in you a spider's web is stronger than a brick wall.

We all face times of great trouble. When we do, it is so easy to forget the victories that God would work in our lives, sometimes in the most surprising ways. Whatever is happening in your life, with God's grace, a mere spider's web can become a brick wall of protection. Believe He is with you always and you will see His great power and love for you.

Our lives are like the course of the sun. At the darkest moment there is the promise of daylight.

* * *

F-E-A-R has two meanings:
1. *Forget everything and run*
2. *Face everything and rise!*

* * *

The greatest Joy	*Giving*
The most effective sleeping pill	*Peace of mind*
The most powerful force in life	*Love*
The two most power-filled words	*"I Can"*
The most beautiful attire	*Smile*

Attitude

One day a farmer's donkey fell down into a well. The animal cried piteously for hours as the farmer tried to figure out what to do. Finally, he decided the animal was old, and the well needed to be covered up anyway; it just wasn't worth it to retrieve the donkey.

He invited all his neighbors to come over and help him. They all grabbed a shovel and began to shovel dirt into the well. At first, the donkey realized what was happening and cried horribly. Then, tired and resigned, he quieted down.

A few shovel loads later, the farmer finally looked down the well. He was astonished at what he saw. With each shovel of dirt that hit his back, the donkey was doing something amazing. He would shake it off and take a step up.

As the farmer's neighbors continued to shovel dirt on top of the animal, he would shake it off and take a step up. Pretty soon, everyone was amazed as the donkey stepped up over the edge of the well and happily trotted off!

Moral: Life is going to shovel dirt on you, all kinds of dirt. The trick to getting out of the well is to shake it off and take a step up. Each of our troubles is a stepping stone. We can get out of the deepest wells just by not stopping, never giving up. Shake it off and take a step up!

Your attitude determines your altitude.

Coffee Beans

A young boy went to his father and told him about his life and how things were so hard for him. He did not know how he was going to make it and wanted to give up. He was tired of fighting and struggling. It seemed as one problem was solved, a new one arose.

His father took him to the kitchen. He filled three pots with water; in the first he placed carrots, in the second he placed eggs, and in the last he put some coffee beans. He let them boil, without saying a word. In about twenty minutes he turned off the burners.

Then he asked his son to feel the carrots. The son did and noted that they were soft. The Father then asked him to take an egg and break it. After pulling off the shell, he observed the hard-boiled egg. Finally, the father asked him to sip the coffee.

The son tasted it and asked, "What does it mean?"

Father explained that each of these objects had faced the same adversity: boiling water. Each reacted differently.

The carrot went in strong, hard, and unrelenting. However, after being subjected to the boiling water, it softened and became weak.

The egg had been fragile. Its thin outer shell had protected its liquid interior, but after sitting through the boiling water, its inside became hardened.

The coffee beans were unique, however. After they were in the boiling water, they had changed the water.

"Which are you?" Father asked him. "When adversity knocks on your door, how do you respond? Are you a carrot, an egg or a coffee bean?"

Think of this: Which am I?

Am I the carrot that seemed strong, but with pain and adversity it became soft and lost its strength?

Am I the egg that starts with a soft heart, but changes with the heat? Did I have a fluid spirit, but after a death, a breakup, a financial hardship or some other trial, have I become hardened and stiff? Does my shell look the same, but on the inside am I bitter and tough with a stiff spirit and hardened heart?

Or am I like the coffee beans? The bean actually changes the hot water, the very circumstance that brings the pain. When the water gets hot, it releases the fragrance and flavor. If you are like the bean, when things are at their worst, you get better and change the situation around you.

How do you handle adversity? When the hour is the darkest and trials are greatest, do you elevate yourself to another level? Are you a carrot, an egg or coffee bean?

The fragrance of flowers spreads only in the direction of the wind. But the goodness of a person spreads in all directions.

Should You be Reacting or Responding to a Situation?

Three women met. Yeah you can guess; exchange of news, views and loads of information! Suddenly, a cockroach flew from nowhere and sat on one of them. She started screaming out of fear. With panic stricken face and trembling voice, she started doing stationary jumping , with both her hands desperately trying to get rid of the cockroach. Her reaction was contagious, as everyone in her group got cranky to what was happening. The lady finally managed to push the cockroach to another lady in the group. Now, it was the turn of the other lady in the group to continue the jumping. The waiter rushed forward to their rescue. In the relay of throwing, the cockroach next fell upon the waiter. The waiter stood firm, composed himself and observed the behavior of the cockroach on his shirt. When he was confident enough, he grabbed and threw it out with his fingers.

Sipping my coffee and watching the amusement, the antenna of my mind picked up a few thoughts and started wondering, "was the cockroach responsible for their histrionic behavior? If so, then why was the waiter not disturbed? He handled it near to perfection, without any chaos. It is not the cockroach, but the inability of the ladies to handle the disturbance caused by the cockroach that disturbed the ladies."

I realized even in my case then, it is not the shouting of my father or my boss that disturbs me, but it's my inability to handle the disturbances caused by their shouting that disturbs me. It's not the traffic jams on the road that disturbs me, but my inability to handle the disturbance caused by the traffic jam that disturbs me. More than the problem, it's my reaction to the problem that hurts me.

Lessons learnt from the story:

I understood, "I should not react in life. I should always respond." The women reacted, whereas the waiter responded. Reactions are always instinctive whereas responses are always intellectual.

Whatever your suffering, whatever your pain,

There will always be sunshine, after the rain.

Perhaps you may stumble, perhaps even fall,

But God's always ready, to answer your call.

He knows every heartache, sees every tear,

A word from His lips, can calm every fear.

Your sorrows may linger, throughout the night,

But suddenly vanish, in dawn's early light.

The Savior is waiting, somewhere above,

To give you His grace, and send you His love.

Whatever your suffering, whatever your pain,

God always sends rainbows, after the rain.

Take off Your Blindfold

His dad takes him into the forest, blindfolded, and leaves him. He was required to sit on a stump the whole night and not to take off the blindfold until the rays of sun shine through it. He cannot cry out for help to anyone.

Once he survives the night he is a man. He cannot tell the other boys of this experience. Each lad must come into his own manhood. The boy was terrified and could hear all kinds of noise. Beasts were all around him; maybe even some human would hurt him. The wind blew the grass, and it shook his stump, but he sat stoically, never removing the blindfold. It was the only way he could become a man.

Finally, after a horrific night, the sound of the night disappeared; he could feel the warmth of the sun. He removed his blindfold. It was then that he saw his father sitting on the stump next to him, keeping watch the entire night.

We are never alone. Even when we do not know it, God is always sitting on the stump beside us to watch and protect us; all we have to do is to take off our blindfolds.

When problems seem to be chasing you, don't try to run away. Turn around in your God-given strength and face them calmly and confidently, knowing that He who is within you is greater than any outer circumstances.

Proper Resource Utilization

Buddha, one day, was in deep thought about the worldly activities and the ways of instilling goodness in human beings. One of his disciples approached him and said humbly "Oh my teacher! While you are so much concerned about the world and others, why don't you look in to the welfare and needs of your own disciples also."

Buddha: "OK. Tell me how I can help you."

Disciple: "Master! My attire is worn out and is beyond the decency to wear the same. Can I get a new one, please?"

Buddha found the robe indeed was in a bad condition and needed replacement. He asked the store keeper to give the disciple a new robe to wear. The disciple thanked Buddha and retired to his room. A while later, Buddha went to his disciple's place and asked him "Is your new attire comfortable? Do you need anything more?"

Disciple: "Thank you my Master. The attire is indeed very comfortable. I need nothing more."

Buddha: "Having got the new one, what did you do with your old attire?"

Disciple: "I am using it as my bedspread."

Buddha: "Then.. hope you have disposed off your old bedspread."

Disciple: "No.. no.. master. I am using my old bedspread as my window curtain."

Buddha: "What about your old curtain?"

Disciple: "Being used to handle hot utensils in the kitchen."

Buddha: "Oh.. I see. Can you tell me what did they do with the old cloth they used in kitchen."

Disciple: "They are being used to wash the floor."

Buddha: "Then, the old rug being used to wash the floor...?"

Disciple: "Master, since they were torn off so much, we could not find any better use, but to use as a twig in the oil lamp, which is right now lit in your study room...."

Buddha smiled in contentment and left for his room.

If not to this degree of utilization, can we at least attempt to find the best use of all our resources at home and in office?

We need to handle wisely, all the resources earth has bestowed us with, both natural and material, so that they can be saved for the generations to come.

Empty pockets teach you a million things in life. But full pockets may spoil you in a million ways.

* * *

Live simply

Love generously

Care deeply

Speak kindly.

God does not Exist

A man went to a barbershop to have his hair cut and his beard trimmed. As the barber began to work, they began to have a good conversation. They talked about so many things on various subjects. When they eventually touched on the subject of God, the barber said: "I don't believe that God exists."

"Why do you say that?" asked the customer.

"Well, you just have to go out in the street to realize that God doesn't exist. Tell me, if God exists, would there be so many sick people? Would there be abandoned children? If God existed, there would be neither suffering nor pain. I can't imagine loving a God who would allow all of these things."

The customer thought for a moment, but didn't respond because he didn't want to start an argument. The barber finished his job and the customer left the shop. Just after he left the barber shop, he saw a man in the street with long, stringy, dirty hair and an untrimmed beard. He looked dirty and un-kept.

The customer turned back and entered the barber shop again and he said to the barber: "You know what? Barbers do not exist."

"How can you say that?" asked the surprised barber. "I am here, and I am a barber. And I just worked on you!"

"No!" the customer exclaimed. "Barbers don't exist because if they did, there would be no people with dirty long hair and untrimmed beards, like that man outside."

"Ah, but barbers do exist! What happens is, people do not come to them."

"Exactly!" affirmed the customer. "That's the point! God, too, does exist! What happens is, people don't go to Him and do not look for Him. That's why there's so much pain and suffering in the world."

May God Give You...

For every storm, a rainbow,

For every tear, a smile,

For every trouble, a promise,

For every trial, a blessing.

For every problem life sends,

A faithful friend to share,

For every sigh, a sweet song,

And an answer for each prayer.

The Aging Phenomena

Do you realize that the only time in our lives when we like to get old is when we're kids? If you're less than 10 years old, you're so excited about aging that you think in fractions. How old are you?.... "I'm four and a half" ....You're never 36 and a half....you're four and a half going on five!

That's the key. You get into your teens, now they can't hold you back. You jump to the next number. How old are you? "I'm gonna be 16." You could be 12, but you're gonna be 16.

And then the greatest day of your life happens....you become 21. Even the words sound like a ceremony....you become 21...YES!!!

But then you turn 30....ooohhh what happened there? Makes you sound like bad milk....He turned 30, we had to throw him out. There's no fun now.

What's wrong?? What changed?? You become 21, you turn 30, then you're pushing 40.....stay over there, it's all slipping away........

You become 21, you turn 30, you're pushing 40, you reach 50.....and your dreams are gone.

Then you make it to 60.....you didn't think you'd make it!

So you become 21, you turn 30, you're pushing 40, you reach 50, you make it to 60......then you build up so much speed you hit 70!

After that, it's a day by day thing. After that, you hit Wednesday.... You get into your 80's, you hit lunch. You turn 85, and you won't even buy grocery for a week ... it's an investment you know, and maybe a bad one.

And it doesn't end there....into the 90's you start going backwards.... I was just 92...

Then a strange thing happens. If you make it over 100, you become a little kid again.... "I'm 100 and a half!"

The Best Gifts to Give...

To your friend ...	LOYALTY
To your enemy ...	FORGIVENESS
To your boss ...	SERVICE
To a child ...	A GOOD EXAMPLE
To your parents ...	GRATITUDE & DEVOTION
To your mate ...	LOVE & FAITHFULNESS
To all men and women ...	LOVE
To yourself ...	RESPECT
To God ...	YOUR LIFE

The Art of Giving

When should One Give?

We all know the famous incident from Mahabharat. Yudhisthir asks a beggar seeking alms to come the next day. On this, Bhim rejoices that Yudhisthir his brother, has conquered death! For he is sure that he will be around the next day to give. Yudhisthir gets the message. One does not know really whether one will be there tomorrow to give! The time to give therefore is now.

How much to Give?

One recalls the famous incident from history. Rana Pratap was reeling after defeat from the Mughals. He had lost his army, he had lost his wealth, and most important, he had lost hope, his will to fight. At that time, in his darkest hour, his erstwhile minister, Bhamasha, came seeking him and placed his entire fortune at the disposal of Rana Pratap. With this, Rana Pratap raised an army and lived to fight another day. The answer to this question how much to give is: "Give as much as one can!"

What to Give?

It is not only money that can be given away. It could be a flower or even a smile. It is not how much one gives but how one gives that really matters. When you give a smile to a stranger that may be the only good thing received by him in days and weeks!

Whom to Give?

Many times we avoid giving by finding fault with the person who is seeking. However, being judgmental and rejecting a

30

person on the presumption that he may not be the most deserving is not justified. "Give without being judgmental!"

How to Give?

Coming to the manner of giving, one has to ensure that the receiver does not feel humiliated, nor the giver feels proud by giving.

In giving, follow the advice 'Let not your left hand know what your right hand gives?' Charity without publicity and fanfare is the highest form of charity. Give with grace and with a feeling of gratitude. 'Give quietly!'

What should One Feel after Giving?

We all know the story of Eklavya. When Dronacharya asked him for his right thumb as *Guru Dakshina*, he unhesitatingly cut off the thumb and gave it to Dronacharya. There is a little known sequel to this story. Eklavya was asked whether he ever regretted the act of giving away his thumb. He replied, and the reply has to be believed to be true, as it was asked to him when he was dying.

His reply was "Yes! I regretted this only once in my life. It was when Pandavas were coming in to kill Dronacharya, who was broken hearted on the false news of death of his son, Ashwathama, and had stopped fighting. It was then that I regretted the loss of my thumb. If the thumb was there, no one could have dared hurt my Guru."

How much should We Provide for Our Heirs?

Ask yourself 'are we taking away from them the gift of work? A source of happiness?' The answer is given by Warren Buffett: "Leave your kids enough to do anything, but not enough to do nothing!"

Why Women are so Special

Mum and Dad were watching TV when Mum said, "I'm tired, and it's getting late. I think I'll go to bed."

She went to the kitchen to make sandwiches for the next day's breakfast. Rinsed out the fruit bowls, checked the cereal box levels, filled the sugar container, put spoons and bowls on the table and refilled the coffee pot for brewing the next morning. She then put some wet clothes in the dryer, put a load of clothes into the washer, ironed a shirt and secured a loose button. She picked up the game pieces left on the table, put the phone back on the charger and put the phone book into the drawer. She emptied a waste-basket and hung up a towel to dry. She yawned and stretched and headed for the bedroom. She stopped by the desk and wrote a note to the teacher, counted out some cash for the excursion and pulled a textbook out from hiding under the chair. She signed a birthday card for a friend, addressed and stamped the envelope and wrote a quick note for the grocery store. She put both near her bag. Mum then washed her face with 3 in 1 cleanser, put on her age fighting moisturizer, brushed and flossed her teeth and filed her nails.

Dad called out, "I thought you were going to bed."

"I'm on my way," she said. She made sure the doors were locked and the patio light was on. She looked in on each of the kids and turned out their bedside lamps, hung up a shirt, threw some dirty socks into the hamper, and had a brief conversation with the one up still doing homework.

In her own room, she set the alarm, laid out clothing for the next day, straightened up the shoe rack. She said her prayers, and visualized the accomplishment of her goals.

About that time, Dad turned off the TV and announced to no one in particular. "I'm going to bed." And he did ... without another thought.

Anything extraordinary here? Wonder why women live longer?

Because they can't die sooner, they still have things to do!!!!

I once had a friend who grew to be very close to me.

Once when we were sitting at the edge of a swimming pool, she filled the palm of her hand with some water and held it before me, and said this: "You see this water carefully contained in my hand? It symbolizes Love."

As long as you keep your hand caringly open and allow it to remain there, it will always be there. However, if you attempt to close your fingers around it and try to possess it, it will spill through the first cracks it finds.

This is the greatest mistake that people do when they meet love...they try to possess it, they demand, they expect... and just like the water spilling out of your hand, love will retrieve from you.

For love is meant to be free, you cannot change its nature. If there are people you love, allow them to be free beings.

Life is beautiful. Live it!!!

The Cab Ride

I arrived at the address and honked the horn. After waiting for a few minutes I walked to the door and knocked. 'Just a minute', answered a frail, elderly voice. I could hear something being dragged across the floor.

After a long pause, the door opened. A small woman in her 90's stood before me. She was wearing a print dress and a pillbox hat with a veil pinned on it, like somebody out of a 1940's movie.

By her side was a small nylon suitcase. 'Would you carry my bag out to the car?' she said. I took the suitcase to the cab, then returned to assist the woman. She took my arm and we walked slowly towards the cab.

She kept thanking me for my kindness. 'It's nothing', I told her. 'I just try to treat my passengers the way I would want my mother to be treated.'

'Oh, you're such a good boy', she said. When we got in the cab, she gave me an address and then asked, 'Could you drive through downtown?'

'It's not the shortest way,' I answered quickly.

'Oh, I don't mind,' she said. 'I'm in no hurry. I'm on my way to a hospice.'

I looked in the rear-view mirror. Her eyes were glistening. 'I don't have any family left,' she continued in a soft voice. 'The doctor says I don't have very long.'

I quietly reached over and shut off the meter. 'What route would you like me to take?' I asked.

For the next two hours, we drove through the city. She showed me the building where she had once worked. We drove through the neighborhood where she and her husband had lived when they were newlyweds. She had me pull up in front of a furniture warehouse that had once been a ballroom where she had gone dancing as a girl.

Sometimes she'd ask me to slow down in front of a particular building or corner and would sit staring into the darkness, saying nothing.

As the first hint of sun was creasing the horizon, she suddenly said, 'I'm tired. Let's go now.'

We drove in silence to the address she had given me. It was a low building, like a small convalescent home, with a driveway that passed under a portico.

Two orderlies came out to the cab as soon as we pulled up. They were solicitous and polite, watching her every move. They must have been expecting her.

I opened the trunk and took the small suitcase to the door. The woman was already seated in a wheelchair.

'How much do I owe you?' She asked, reaching into her purse.

'Nothing,' I said.

'You have to make a living,' she answered.

'There are other passengers,' I responded.

Almost without thinking, I bent and gave her a hug. She held onto me tightly.

'You gave an old woman a little moment of joy,' she said. 'Thank you.'

I squeezed her hand, and then walked into the dim light. Behind me, a door shut. It was the sound of the closing of a life.

I didn't pick up any more passengers that shift. I drove aimlessly lost in thought. For the rest of that day, I could hardly talk. What if that woman had gotten an angry driver, or one who was impatient to end his shift?

What if I had refused to take the run, or had honked once, then driven away?

On a quick review, I don't think that I have done anything more important in my life.

We're conditioned to think that our lives revolve around great moments.

But great moments often catch us unaware—beautifully wrapped in what others may consider a small one.

Great opportunities to help others seldom come, but small ones surround us every day.

* * *

Kindness is a language the deaf can hear, the blind can see and the mute can speak.

* * *

The smallest good deed is better than the grandest good intention.

The Savings Account

Meena married Rahul. At the end of the wedding party, Meena's mother gave her a newly opened bank saving passbook with ₹ 10,000 deposit amount.

Mother: "Meena, take this passbook. Keep it as a record of your married life. When something happy and memorable happens in your new life, put some money in. Write down what it's about next to the line. The more memorable the event is, the more money you can put in. I've done the first one for you today. Do the others with Rahul. When you look back after years, you can know how much happiness you've had."

Meena shared this with Rahul. They both thought it was a great idea and were anxious to know when the second deposit can be made.

This was what they did after some time:

- 7 Feb: ₹ 3000, first birthday celebration for Rahul after marriage

- 1 Mar: ₹ 1000, salary raise for Meena

- 20 Mar: ₹ 2000, vacation trip to Bali

- 15 Apr: ₹ 10,000, Meena got pregnant

- 1 Jun: ₹ 2000, Rahul got promoted

.... and so on...

However, after years, they started fighting and arguing for trivial things. They didn't talk much. They regretted that they had married the most nasty person in the world.... no more love.

One day Meena talked to her Mother: "Mom, we can't stand it anymore. We have agreed to divorce. I can't imagine how I decided to marry this guy."

Mother: "Sure, dear, that's no big deal. Just do whatever you want if you really can't stand it. But before that, do one thing first. Remember the saving passbook I gave you on your wedding day? Take out all money and spend it first. You shouldn't keep any record of such a poor marriage."

Meena thought it was a good advice. So she went to the bank, waiting in the queue and planning to cancel the account. While she was waiting, she took a look at the passbook record. She looked, and looked, and looked. Then the memory of all the previous joy and happiness just came up her mind. Her eyes were then filled with tears. She left and went home. When she was home, she handed the passbook to Rahul and asked him to spend the money before getting the divorce.

The next day, Rahul gave the passbook back to Meena. She found a new deposit of ₹ 15,000. And a line next to the record: "This is the day I notice how much I've loved you throughout all these years. How much happiness you've brought me."

They hugged and cried, putting the passbook back in the safe.

Love is the only flower that grows and blossoms without the aid of seasons.

The Test of Three

In ancient Greece (469–399 BC), Socrates was widely lauded for his wisdom. One day the great philosopher came upon an acquaintance who ran up to him excitedly and said, "Socrates, do you know what I just heard about one of your students?"

"Wait a moment," Socrates replied. "Before you tell me I'd like you to pass a little test. It's called the Test of Three."

"Test of Three?"

"That's right," Socrates continued. "Before you talk to me about my student, let's take a moment to test what you're going to say. The first test is *Truth*. Have you made absolutely sure that what you are about to tell me is true?"

"No," the man said, "actually I just heard about it."

"All right," said Socrates. "So you don't really know if it's true or not. Now let's try the second test, the test of *Goodness*. Is what you are about to tell me about my student something good?"

"No, on the contrary..."

"So," Socrates continued, "you want to tell me something bad about him even though you're not certain it's true?"

The man shrugged, a little embarrassed.

Socrates continued. "You may still pass though, because there is a third test—the filter of *Usefulness*. Is what you want to tell me about my student going to be useful to me?"

"No, not really."

"Well," concluded Socrates, "if what you want to tell me is neither *True* nor *Good* nor even *Useful*, why tell it to me at all?"

The man was defeated and ashamed. This is the reason Socrates was held in such high esteem.

If You Want Happiness

For an hour........................... *Eat good food*

For a day .... *Go for a picnic*

For a month .... *Go for a long vacation*

For a year.............................. *Inherit a fortune*

For many years...................... *Love someone*

For a lifetime .... *Help someone*

* * *

The perfect universe is here now, but it takes perfect vision to see it.

* * *

Knowledge is proud that he has learned so much;

Wisdom is humble that he knows no more.

40

Weakness or Strength

Sometimes your biggest weakness can become your biggest strength. Take, for example, the story of one 10-year-old boy who decided to study judo despite the fact that he had lost his left arm in a devastating car accident.

The boy began lessons with an old Japanese judo master. The boy was doing well, so he couldn't understand why, after three months of training the master had taught him only one move.

"Sensei," the boy finally said, "Shouldn't I be learning more moves?"

"This is the only move you know, but this is the only move you'll ever need to know," the sensei replied.

Not quite understanding, but believing in his teacher, the boy kept training.

Several months later, the sensei took the boy to his first tournament. Surprising himself, the boy easily won his first two matches. The third match proved to be more difficult, but after some time, his opponent became impatient and charged; the boy deftly used his one move to win the match. Still amazed by his success, the boy was now in the finals.

This time, his opponent was bigger, stronger, and more experienced. For a while, the boy appeared to be over-matched. Concerned that the boy might get hurt, the referee called a time-out. He was about to stop the match when the sensei intervened.

"No," the sensei insisted, "let him continue."

Soon after the match resumed, his opponent made a critical mistake, he dropped his guard. Instantly, the boy used his move to pin him. The boy had won the match and the tournament. He was the champion.

On the way home, the boy and sensei reviewed every move in each and every match. Then the boy summoned the courage to ask what was really on his mind.

"Sensei, how did I win the tournament with only one move?"

"You won for two reasons," the sensei answered. "First, you've almost mastered one of the most difficult throws in all of judo. And second, the only known defence for that move is for your opponent to grip your left arm."

The boy's biggest weakness had become his biggest strength.

Nothing is "Impossible" in this World, As the word Impossible itself means

"I M POSSIBLE"

* * *

Winning does not always mean being first; winning means you are doing better than you have done before.

* * *

By failing to prepare, you are preparing to fail.

Wealth, Success and Love

A woman came out of her house and saw three old men with long white beards sitting in her front yard. She did not recognize them. She said "I don't think I know you, but you must be hungry. Please come in and have something to eat."

"Is the man of the house home?" they asked.

"No", she replied. "He's out."

"Then we cannot come in", they replied.

In the evening when her husband came home, she told him what had happened.

"Go tell them I am home and invite them in."

The woman went out and invited the men in.

"We do not go into a house together," they replied.

"Why is that?" she asked.

One of the old men explained: "His name is Wealth," he said pointing to one of his friends, and said pointing to another one, "He is Success, and I am Love." Then he added, "Now go in and discuss with your husband which one of us you want in your home."

The woman went in and told her husband what was said. Her husband was overjoyed. "How nice!" he said. "Since that is the case, let us invite Wealth. Let him come and fill our home with wealth!"

His wife disagreed. "My dear, why don't we invite Success?"

Their daughter was listening from the other corner of the house. She jumped in with her own suggestion: "Would it not be better to invite Love? Our home will then be filled with love!"

"Let us heed our daughter's advice," said the husband to his wife.

"Go out and invite Love to be our guest."

The woman went out and asked the three old men, "Which one of you is Love? Please come in and be our guest."

Love got up and started walking towards the house. The other two also got up and followed him. Surprised, the lady asked Wealth and Success: "I only invited Love, why are you coming in?"

The old men replied together: "If you had invited Wealth or Success, the other two of us would've stayed out, but since you invited Love, wherever He goes, we go with him. Wherever there is Love, there is also Wealth and Success!!!"

Mistakes are painful when they happen.

But year's later collection of mistakes is called experience, which leads to success.

Be bold when you loose and be calm when you win.

Heated gold becomes ornament.

Beaten copper becomes wires.

Depleted stone becomes statue.

So the more pain you get in life you become more valuable.

What do You do all Day?

A man came home from work and found his three children outside, still in their pyjamas, playing in the mud, with empty food boxes and 20 wrappers strewn all around the front yard.

The door of his wife's car was open, and so the front door to the house and there was no sign of the dog. Proceeding into the entry, he found an even bigger mess. A lamp had been knocked over, and the throw rug was wadded against one wall.

In the front room the TV was loudly blaring a cartoon channel, and the family room was strewn with toys and various items of clothing.

In the kitchen, dishes filled the sink, breakfast food was spilled on the counter, the fridge door was open wide, dog food was spilled on the floor, a broken glass lay under the table, and a small pile of sand was spread by the back door.

He quickly headed up the stairs, stepping over toys and more piles of clothes, looking for his wife. He was worried she might be ill, or that something serious had happened.

He was met with a small trickle of water as it made its way out of the bathroom door.

As he peered inside he found wet towels, scummy soap and more toys thrown over the floor. Miles of toilet paper lay in a heap and tooth paste had been smeared over the mirror and walls.

As he rushed to the bedroom, he found his wife still curled up in the bed in her pyjamas, reading a novel.

She looked up at him, smiled, and asked how his day went.

He looked at her bewildered and asked, "What happened here today?"

She again smiled and answered, "You know every day when you come home from work and you ask me what in the world I do all day?"

"Yes," was his incredulous reply.

She answered, "Well, today I didn't do it..."

An archeologist is the best husband any woman can have;

The older she gets, the more interested he is in her.

* * *

Easy is to judge the mistakes of others.

Difficult is to recognize our own mistakes.

* * *

Never feel bad if people remember you at the time of their need. Feel privileged that they think of you like a candle in the darkness of their life.

* * *

Everybody thinks of changing humanity, but nobody thinks of changing himself.

The Important Things in Life

A philosophy professor stood before his class with some items on the table in front of him. When the class began, wordlessly he picked up a very large and empty jar and proceeded to fill it with rocks, about 2 inches in diameter.

He then asked the students if the jar was full. They agreed that it was.

So the professor then picked up a box of pebbles and poured them into the jar. He shook the jar lightly. The pebbles, of course, rolled into the open areas between the rocks.

He then asked the students again if the jar was full. They agreed it was.

The professor picked up a box of sand and poured it into the jar. Of course, the sand filled up everything else.

He then asked once more if the jar was full. The students responded with a unanimous "Yes".

"Now", said the professor, "I want you to recognize that this jar represents your life. The rocks are the important things—your family, your partner, your health, your children—things that if everything else was lost and only they remained, your life would still be full."

"The pebbles are the other things that matter—like your job, your house, your car."

"The sand is everything else. The small stuff. If you put the sand into the jar first," he continued "there is no room for the pebbles or the rocks. The same goes for your life."

"If you spend all your time and energy on the small stuff, you will never have room for the things that are important to you. Pay attention to the things that are critical to your happiness. Play with your children. Take your partner out dancing. There will always be time to go to work, clean the house, give a dinner party and fix the disposal."

"Take care of the rocks first—the things that really matter. Set your priorities. The rest is just sand."

Challenges are high

The Dreams are new

The World out there

Is waiting for you.

Dare to Dream

Dare to Try

No Goal is too distant

No Star is too high.

A to Z of Life

A—Accept

Accept others for who they are and for the choices they've made even if you have difficulty understanding their beliefs, motives, or actions.

B—Break Away

Break away from everything that stands in the way of what you hope to accomplish with your life.

C—Create

Create a family of friends whom you can share your hopes, dreams, sorrows, and happiness with.

D—Decide

Decide that you'll be successful and happy come what may, and good things will find you. The roadblocks are only minor obstacles along the way.

E—Explore

Explore and experiment. The world has much to offer, and you have much to give. And every time you try something new, you'll learn more about yourself.

F—Forgive

Forgive and forget. Grudges only weigh you down and inspire unhappiness and grief. Soar above it, and remember that everyone makes mistakes.

G—Grow

Leave the past mistakes behind. They can no longer hurt you or stand in your way.

H—Hope

Hope for the best and never forget that anything is possible as long as you remain dedicated to the task.

I—Ignore

Ignore the negative voice inside your head. Focus instead on your goals and remember your accomplishments. Your past success is only a small inkling of what the future holds.

J—Journey

Journey to new worlds, new possibilities, by remaining open-minded. Try to learn something new every day, and you'll grow.

K—Know

Know that no matter how bad things seem, they'll always get better. The warmth of spring always follows the harshest winter.

L—Love

Let love fill your heart instead of hate. When hate is in your heart, there's room for nothing else, but when love is in your heart, there's room for endless happiness.

M—Manage

Manage your time and your expenses wisely, and you'll suffer less stress and worry. Then you'll be able to focus on the important things in life.

N—Notice

Never ignore the poor, infirm, helpless, weak, or suffering. Offer your assistance when possible, and always your kindness and understanding.

O—Open

Open your eyes and take in all the beauty around you. Even during the worst of times, there's still much to be thankful for.

P—Play

Never forget to have fun along the way. Success means nothing without happiness.

Q—Question

Ask many questions, because you're here to learn.

R—Relax

Refuse to let worry and stress rule your life, and remember that things always have a way of working out in the end.

S—Share

Share your talent, skills, knowledge, and time with others. Everything that you invest in others will return to you many times over.

T—Try

Even when your dreams seem impossible to reach, try anyway. You'll be amazed by what you can accomplish.

U—Use

Use your gifts to your best ability. Talent that's wasted has no value. Talent that's used will bring unexpected rewards.

V—Value

Value the friends and family members who've supported and encouraged you, and be there for them as well.

W—Work

Work hard every day to be the best person you can be, but never feel guilty if you fall short of your goals. Every sunrise offers a second chance.

X—X-Ray

Like X-ray, look deep inside the hearts of those around you and you'll see the goodness and beauty within.

Y—Yield

Yield to commitment. If you stay on track and remain dedicated, you'll find success at the end of the road.

Z—Zoom

Zoom to a happy place when bad memories or sorrow rears its ugly head. Let nothing interfere with your goals. Instead, focus on your abilities, your dreams, and a brighter tomorrow.

Why Me?

Arthur Ashe, the legendary wimbledon player was diagnosed with aids. From world over, he received letters from his fans, one of which said: "Why does God have to select you for such a bad disease?" To this Arthur Ashe replied: The world over, 5 crore children start playing tennis, 50 lakh learn to play tennis, 5 lakh learn professional tennis, 50000 come to the circuit. 5000 reach the grand slam, 50 reach wimbledon, 4 to semifinal, 2 to the finals. When I was holding a cup I never asked God, "Why me?" And today in pain I should not be asking God, "Why me?"

The Pencil Story

The pencil maker took the pencil aside, just before putting it into the box.

He told the pencil, "There are 5 things you need to know, before I send you out into the world. Always remember them and never forget, and you will become the best pencil you can be."

One: You will be able to do many great things, but only if you allow yourself to be held in someone's hand.

Two: You will experience a painful sharpening from time to time, but you'll need it to become a better pencil.

Three: You will be able to correct any mistakes you might make.

Four: The most important part of you will always be what's inside.

Five: On every surface you are used on, you must leave your mark. No matter what the condition, you must continue to write.

The pencil understood and promised to remember, and went into the box with purpose in its heart.

* * *

Now replacing the place of the pencil with you. Always remember them and never forget, and you will become the best person you can be.

One: You will be able to do many great things, but only if you allow yourself to be held in God's hand. And allow other human beings to access you for the many gifts you possess.

Two: You will experience a painful sharpening from time to time, by going through various problems in life, but you'll need it to become a stronger person.

Three: You will be able to correct any mistakes you might make.

Four: The most important part of you will always be what's on the inside.

Five: On every surface you walk through, you must leave your mark. No matter what the situation, you must continue to do your duties.

Allow this parable on the pencil to encourage you to know that you are a special person and only you can fulfill the purpose to which you were born to accomplish.

Never allow yourself to get discouraged. Your life is significant and can make a change.

Every successful person has a painful story.

Every painful story has a successful ending.

Accept the pain and get ready for success.

Miracle

A little girl, Neha, went to her bedroom and pulled a glass jelly jar from its hiding place in the closet. She poured the change out on the floor and counted it carefully. Placing the coins back in the jar and twisting on the cap, she slipped out the back door and made her way to Sood Drug Store.

She waited patiently for the pharmacist to give her some attention but he was too busy at this moment. Neha twisted her feet to make a scuffing noise. Nothing. She cleared her throat with the most disgusting sound she could muster. No good. Finally, she took a coin from her jar and banged it on the glass counter. That did it!

"And what do you want?" the pharmacist asked in an annoyed tone of voice. "I'm busy with my brother from abroad whom I am meeting after ages," he said without waiting for a reply to his question.

"Well, I want to talk to you about my brother," Neha answered back in the same annoyed tone. "He's really, really sick... and I want to buy a miracle."

"I beg your pardon?" said the pharmacist.

"His name is Dhruv and he has something bad growing inside his head and my Daddy says only a miracle can save him now. So how much does a miracle cost?"

"We don't sell miracles here, little girl. I'm sorry but I can't help you", the pharmacist said, softening a little.

"Listen, I have the money to pay for it. If it isn't enough, I will get more. Just tell me how much it costs."

The pharmacist's brother was a well dressed man. He stooped down and asked the little girl, "What kind of a miracle does your brother need?"

"I don't know," Neha replied with her eyes welling up. "I just know he's really sick and Mommy says he needs an operation. But my Daddy can't pay for it, so I want to use my money."

"How much do you have?" asked the man from abroad.

"One hundred and seventy rupees," Neha answered, barely audible. "And it's all the money I have, but I can get some more if I need to."

"Well, what a coincidence," smiled the man. "One hundred and seventy rupees—the exact price of a miracle for little brothers."

He took her money in one hand and with the other hand he grasped her little hand and said, "Take me to where you live. I want to see your brother and meet your parents. Let's see if I have the miracle you need."

That well dressed man was Dr. Sood, a surgeon, specializing in neuro-surgery. The operation was completed free of charge and it wasn't long until Dhruv was home again and doing well.

Mom and Dad were happily talking about the chain of events that had led them to this place.

"That surgery," her Mom whispered. "was a real miracle. I wonder how much it would have cost?"

Neha smiled. She knew exactly how much does a miracle cost—one hundred and seventy rupees—plus the faith of a little child.

Never Judge Anyone by their Appearance

A lady in a faded dress and her husband, dressed in a homespun threadbare suit, stepped off the train in Boston, and walked timidly without an appointment into the Harvard University President's outer office.

The secretary could tell in a moment that such backwoods, country hicks had no business at Harvard.

"We'd like to see the president," the man said softly.

"He'll be busy all day," the secretary snapped.

"We'll wait," the lady replied.

For hours the secretary ignored them, hoping that the couple would finally become discouraged and go away.

They didn't, and the secretary grew frustrated and finally decided to disturb the president, even though it was a chore she always regretted.

"Maybe if you see them for a few minutes, they'll leave," she said to him.

He sighed in exasperation and nodded. Someone of his importance obviously didn't have the time to spend with them.

The president, stern faced and with dignity, strutted towards the couple.

The lady told him, "We had a son who attended Harvard for one year. He loved Harvard. He was happy here. But about a year ago, he was accidentally killed. My husband and I would like to erect a memorial to him, somewhere on campus."

The president wasn't touched. He was shocked. "Madam," he said, gruffly, "we can't put up a statue for every person who attended Harvard and died. If we did, this place would look like a cemetery."

"Oh, no," the lady explained quickly. "We don't want to erect a statue. We thought we would like to give a building to Harvard."

The president rolled his eyes. He glanced at the faded dress and homespun suit, and then exclaimed, "A building! Do you have any earthly idea how much a building costs? We have over seven and a half million dollars in the physical buildings here at Harvard."

For a moment the lady was silent. The president was pleased. Maybe he could get rid of them now. The lady turned to her husband and said quietly, "Is that all it costs to start a university? Why don't we just start our own?"

Her husband nodded. The president's face wilted in confusion and bewilderment.

Mr and Mrs Leland Stanford got up and walked away, travelling to Palo Alto, California where they established the university that bears their name, Stanford University, a memorial to a son that Harvard no longer cared about.

If you are planning for a year, sow rice; if you are planning for a decade, plant trees; if you are planning for a lifetime, educate people.

Until Death do Us Apart

When I got home that night as my wife served dinner, I held her hand and said, "I've got something to tell you." She sat down and ate quietly. Suddenly I didn't know how to open my mouth. But I had to let her know what I was thinking. I wanted a divorce. I raised the topic calmly. She didn't seem to be annoyed by my words, instead she asked me softly, "why?" I avoided her question. This made her angry. She threw away the utensils and shouted at me, you are not a man!

That night, we didn't talk to each other. She was weeping. I knew she wanted to find out what had happened to our marriage. But I could hardly give her a satisfactory answer. I had lost my heart to a lovely girl called Lavanya. I didn't love my wife anymore. I just pitied her!

With a deep sense of guilt, I drafted a divorce agreement which stated that she could own our house, 30% shares of my company and the car. She glanced at it and then tore it into pieces. The woman who had spent twelve years of her life with me had become a stranger. I felt sorry for her wasted time, resources and energy but I could not take back what I had said, for I loved Lavanya so dearly.

Finally she cried loudly in front of me, which was what I had expected to see. To me her cry was actually a kind of release. The idea of divorce which had obsessed me for several weeks seemed to be firmer and clearer now.

The next day, I came back home very late and found her writing something at the table. I didn't have dinner, but went straight to sleep and fell asleep very fast because I was tired after an eventful day with Lavanya. When I woke up, she was still there at the table writing. I just did not care so I turned over and was asleep again.

In the morning she presented her divorce conditions: she didn't want anything from me, but needed a month's notice before the divorce. She requested that in that one month we both struggle to live as normal a life as possible. Her reasons were simple. Our son had his exams in a month's time and she didn't want to disturb him with the news of our broken marriage.

This was agreeable to me. But she had something more, she asked me to recall how I had carried her into out bridal room on our wedding day. She requested that everyday for the month's duration I carry her out of our bedroom to the front door every morning. I thought she was going crazy. Just to make our last days together bearable, I accepted her odd request.

I told Lavanya about my wife's divorce conditions. She laughed loudly and thought it was absurd. No matter what tricks she applies, she has to face the divorce, she said scornfully.

My wife and I hadn't had any body contact since my divorce intention was explicitly expressed. So when I carried her out on the first day, we both appeared clumsy. Our son clapped behind us, "daddy is holding mummy in his arms." His words brought me a sense of pain. From the bedroom to the sitting room, then to the door, I walked over ten metres with her in my arms. She closed her eyes and said softly, don't tell our son about the divorce. I nodded, feeling somewhat upset. I put her down outside the door. She went to wait for the bus to work. I drove alone to the office.

On the second day, both of us acted much more easily. She leaned on my chest. I could smell the fragrance of her blouse. I realized that I hadn't looked at this woman carefully for a long time. I realised she was not young any more. There were fine wrinkles on her face, her hair were greying! Our marriage had taken its toll on her. For a minute, I wondered what I had done to her.

On the fourth day, when I lifted her up, I felt a sense of intimacy returning. This was the woman who had given twelve years of her life to me. On the fifth and sixth day, I realized that our sense of intimacy was growing more. I didn't tell Lavanya about this.

It became easier to carry her as the month slipped by. Perhaps the everyday workout made me stronger. She was choosing what to wear one morning. She tried on quite a few dresses but could not find a suitable one. Then she sighed, all my dresses have grown bigger. I suddenly realized that she had grown so thin, that was the reason why I could carry her more easily. Suddenly it hit me...... she had buried so much pain and bitterness in her heart.

Subconsciously, I reached out and touched her head. Our son came in at the moment and said, "Dad, it's time to carry mum out." To him, seeing his father carrying his mother out had become an essential part of his life. My wife gestured to our son to come closer and hugged him tightly. I turned my face away because I was afraid I might change my mind at this last minute. I then held her in my arms, walking from the bedroom, through the sitting room, to the hallway. Her hand surrounded my neck softly and naturally. I held her body tightly, it was just like our wedding day.

But her much lighter weight made me sad. On the last day, when I held her in my arms I could hardly move a step. I hadn't noticed that our life lacked intimacy. I drove to office..... jumped out of the car swiftly without locking the door. I was afraid any delay would make me change my mind. I walked upstairs. Lavanya opened the door and I said to her, "Sorry Lavanya, I do not want the divorce anymore."

She looked at me, astonished. Then touched my forehead. "Do you have a fever?" she asked.

I moved her hand off my head. "Sorry Lavanya...." I said, "I won't divorce. My married life was boring probably because she and I didn't value the details of our lives, not because we didn't love each other any more. Now I realise that since I carried her into my home on our wedding day, I am supposed to hold her until death does us apart."

Lavanya seemed to suddenly wake up. She gave me a loud slap and then slammed the door and burst into tears. I walked downstairs and drove away. At the floral shop on the way, I ordered a bouquet of flowers for my wife. The salesgirl asked me what to write on the card. I smiled and wrote: *I'll carry you out every morning. Until death do us apart.*

True love is not loving a perfect person

but loving an imperfect person perfectly!

Merry Christmas!

Three years ago, a little boy and his grandmother came to see Santa at the Mayfair Mall in Wisconsin. The child climbed up on his lap, holding a picture of a little girl.

"Who is this?" asked Santa, smiling. "Your friend? Your sister?"

"Yes Santa," he replied. "My sister Sarah, who is very sick," he said sadly.

Santa glanced over at the grandmother who was waiting nearby, and saw her dabbing her eyes with a tissue. "She wanted to come to see you, oh, so very much, Santa!" the child exclaimed. "She misses you," he added softly.

Santa tried to be cheerful and encouraged a smile on the boy's face, asking him what he wanted Santa to bring him for Christmas.

When they finished their visit, the Grandmother came over to help the child off his lap, and started to say something to Santa, but halted.

"What is it?" Santa asked warmly.

"Well, I know it's really too much to ask you, Santa, but..." the old woman began, shooing her grandson over to one of Santa's elves to collect the little gift which Santa gave to all his young visitors.

"The girl in the photograph, my granddaughter, well, you see ... she has leukemia and isn't expected to make it even through the holidays," she said through tear-filled eyes. "Is there any way, Santa, any possible way that you could come to see Sarah? That's all she's asked for, for Christmas, is to see Santa."

Santa blinked and swallowed hard and told the woman to leave information with his elves as to where Sarah was, and he would see what he could do.

Santa thought of little else the rest of that afternoon. He knew what he had to do. "What if it were my child lying in that hospital bed, dying," he thought with a sinking heart, "This is the least I can do."

When Santa finished meeting all the boys and girls that evening, he retrieved from his helper the name of the hospital where Sarah was admitted. He asked the assistant location manager how to get to Children's Hospital.

"Why?" Rick asked, with a puzzled look on his face.

Santa relayed to him the conversation with Sarah's grand-mother earlier that day.

"C'mon, I'll take you there," Rick said softly. Rick drove to the hospital and came inside with Santa. They found out which room Sarah was in. A pale Rick said he would wait out in the hall.

Santa quietly peeked into the room through the half-closed door and saw little Sarah on the bed. The room was full of what appeared to be her family; there was the grandmother and the girl's brother he had met earlier that day. A woman whom he guessed was Sarah's mother stood by the bed, gently pushing Sarah's thin hair off her forehead. And another woman who he discovered later was Sarah's aunt, sat in a chair near the bed with a weary, sad look on her face. They were talking quietly, and Santa could sense the warmth and closeness of the family, and their love and concern for Sarah.

Taking a deep breath, and forcing a smile on his face, Santa entered the room, bellowing a hearty, "Ho, Ho, Ho!"

"Santa!" shrieked little Sarah weakly, as she tried to escape her bed to run to him, intravenous tubes intact.

Santa rushed to her side and gave her a warm hug. A child, the tender age of his own son—9 years old—gazed up at him with wonder and excitement.

Her skin was pale and her short tresses bore telltale bald patches from the effects of chemotherapy. But all he saw when he looked at her was a pair of huge, blue eyes. His heart melted, and he had to force himself to choke back tears. Though his eyes were riveted upon Sarah's face, he could hear the gasps and quiet sobbing of the women in the room.

As he and Sarah began talking, the family crept quietly to the bedside, one by one, squeezing Santa's shoulder or his hand gratefully, whispering, "Thank you" as they gazed sincerely at him with shining eyes.

Santa and Sarah talked and talked, and she told him excitedly all the toys she wanted for Christmas, assuring him she'd been a very good girl that year.

As their time together dwindled, Santa felt led in his spirit to pray for Sarah, and asked for permission from the girl's mother. She nodded in agreement and the entire family circled around Sarah's bed, holding hands. Santa looked intensely at Sarah and asked her if she believed in angels.

"Oh yes, Santa. I do!" she exclaimed.

"Well, I'm going to ask that angels watch over you." He said, laying one hand on the child's head. Santa closed his eyes and prayed. He asked that God touch little Sarah, and heal her body from this disease. And when he finished praying, still with eyes closed, he started singing, softly, "Silent Night, Holy Night; All is calm, All is bright."

The family joined in, still holding hands, smiling at Sarah, and crying tears of hope, tears of joy for this moment, as Sarah beamed at them all.

When the song ended, Santa sat on the side of the bed again and held Sarah's frail, small hands in his own. "Now Sarah," he said authoritatively, "you have a job to do, and that is to concentrate on getting well. I want you to have fun playing with your friends this summer, and I expect to see you at my house at Mayfair Mall this time next year!"

He knew it was risky proclaiming that to this little girl who had terminal cancer, but he 'had' to. He had to give her the greatest gift he could—not dolls or games or toys—but the gift of HOPE.

"Yes Santa!" Sarah exclaimed, her eyes bright. He leaned down and kissed her on the forehead and left the room.

Out in the hall, the minute Santa's eyes met Rick's, a look passed between them and they wept unashamed. Sarah's mother and grandmother slipped out of the room quickly and rushed to Santa's side to thank him.

"My only child is the same age as Sarah," he explained quietly. "This is the least I could do." They nodded with understanding and hugged him.

One year later, Santa was back in the same mall for his six-week, seasonal job which he so loved to do. Several weeks went by and then one day a child came up to sit on his lap.

"Hi Santa! Remember me?"

"Of course, I do," Santa proclaimed (as he always does), smiling down at her. After all, the secret to being a 'good' Santa is to always make each child feel as if they are the 'only' child in the world at that moment.

"You came to see me in the hospital last year!"

Santa's jaw dropped. Tears immediately sprang in his eyes, and he grabbed this little miracle and held her to his chest. "Sarah!" he exclaimed.

He scarcely recognized her, for her hair was long and silky and her cheeks were rosy—much different from the little girl he had visited just a year before. He looked over and saw Sarah's mother and grandmother in the sidelines smiling and waving and wiping their eyes.

That was the best Christmas ever for Santa Claus. He had witnessed—and been blessed to be instrumental in bringing about this miracle of hope. This precious little child was healed. Cancer-free, alive and well. He silently looked up to heaven and humbly whispered, "Thank you, Father. This is a very special Christmas!"

In the depth of winter, I finally learned that within me there lay an invincible summer.

The Law of the Seed

Take a look at an apple tree. There might be five hundred apples on the tree, each with ten seeds. That's a lot of seeds!

We might ask, "Why would you need so many seeds to grow just a few more trees?"

Nature has something to teach us here. It's telling us: "Most seeds never grow. So if you really want to make something happen, you better try more than once."

This might mean:

You'll attend twenty interviews to get one job.

You'll interview forty people to find one good employee.

You'll talk to fifty people to sell one house, car, vacuum cleaner, insurance policy, idea...

And you might meet a hundred acquaintances to find one special friend.

When we understand the "Law of the Seed", we don't get so disappointed. We stop feeling like victims. Laws of nature are not things to take personally.

We just need to understand them, and work with them.

> *The illiterate of the present century will not be those who cannot read and write, but those who cannot learn, unlearn, and relearn.*

Are You Good Enough?

A little boy went into a drug store, reached for a soda carton and pulled it over to the telephone. He climbed onto the carton so that he could reach the buttons on the phone and proceeded to punch in the digits.

The store owner listened to the following conversation.

The boy said, "Madam, I want to mow your lawn."

The woman replied, "I already have someone to mow my lawn."

"Madam, I will cut your lawn for half the price of the person who cuts your lawn now."

The woman responded that she was very satisfied with the person who was presently cutting her lawn.

The little boy found more perseverance and offered, "Madam, I'll even sweep your curb and your sidewalk, so on Sunday you will have the prettiest lawn in the entire neighbourhood."

Again the woman answered in the negative. With a smile on his face, the little boy replaced the receiver.

The druggist walked over to the boy and said, "Son, I like your attitude, I like that positive spirit. Son, I would like to offer you a job."

The little boy replied, "No thanks, I was just checking on the job I already have."

What Happens in Heaven

I dreamt that I went to Heaven and an angel was showing me around. We walked side-by-side inside a large workroom filled with angels. My angel guide stopped in front of the first section and said, "This is the Receiving Section. Here all petitions to God said in prayer are received."

I looked around in this area, and it was terribly busy with so many angels sorting out petitions written on voluminous paper sheets and scraps from people all over the world.

Then we moved on down a long corridor until we reached the second section. The angel then said to me, "This is the Packaging and Delivery Section. Here the graces and blessings the people asked for are processed and delivered to the persons who asked for them."

I noticed again how busy it was there. There were many angels working hard at that station, since so many blessings had been requested and were being packaged for delivery to Earth.

Finally at the farthest end of the long corridor we stopped at the door of a very small section. To my great surprise, only one angel was seated there, doing nothing. "This is the Acknowledgment Section," my angel friend quietly admitted to me. He seemed embarrassed. "How is it that there is no work going on here?" I asked.

"So sad," the angel sighed. "After people receive the blessings that they asked for, very few send back acknowledgments."

"What blessings should they acknowledge?" I asked.

"If you have food in the refrigerator, clothes on your back, a roof overhead and a place to sleep, you are richer than 75% of this world. If you have money in the bank, in your wallet, and spare change in a dish, you are among the top 8% of the world's wealthy."

"If you woke up this morning with more health than illness, you are more blessed than the many who will not even survive this day."

"If you can hold your head up and smile, you are not the norm, you're unique to all those in doubt and despair."

"How does one acknowledge God's blessings?" I asked.

"Simple," the angel answered. Just say, "Thank you, Lord."

Worries at the start of the day means you are still alive.

Clothes don't fit means you have a good appetite.

Tears in eyes means there is somebody you care for.

Mess to clean after party means you have friends.

Roof that needs fixing means you have a home.

Taxes to pay means you are not unemployed.

The Law of the Garbage Truck

One day, I hopped into a taxi and took off for the airport. We were driving in the right lane when suddenly, a black car, jumped out of a parking space right in front of us. My taxi driver slammed the brakes, skidded, and missed the other car by just inches!

The driver of the other car whipped his head around and started yelling at us. My taxi driver just smiled and waved at the guy. I mean, he was really friendly.

So I asked, "Why did you do that? This guy almost ruined your car and sent us to the hospital!" This is when my taxi driver taught me what I now call, 'The Law of the Garbage Truck'.

He explained, "Many people are like garbage trucks. They run around full of garbage, full of frustration, full of anger, and full of disappointment. As their garbage piles up, they need a place to dump it and sometimes they'll dump it on you. Never take it personally. Just smile, wave, wish them well, and move on with the routine life. Don't take their garbage and spread it to other people at work, at home or on the streets."

The bottom line is that successful people do not let garbage trucks take over their day. Life's too short to wake up in the morning with regrets, so *love the people who treat you right; pray for the ones who don't.*

> *Life is 10% what you make it and 90% how you take it!*

A Glass of Milk

One day, a poor boy, Shekhar, was selling clothing door to door, to pay for his education and realized that he only had ten rupees left in his pocket. He was hungry, so he decided to ask for some food at the next house that he came to.

He lost his hunger when a beautiful young woman opened the door. Instead of a meal, he asked her for a glass of water. She saw that he was very hungry so she brought him a glass of milk. He drank it very slowly and then asked, "How much do I owe you?"

"You do not owe me anything at all," she replied, "My mother taught us never to accept anything for doing someone a kindness."

Shekhar replied: "Then I thank you from the bottom of my heart." When he left the house, feeling stronger physically, he sensed a return of his faith in the lord which he had nearly abandoned.

Years later, this same young woman fall gravely ill. The local doctors were mystified, so they sent her to the big city where they knew that the specialists would be able to diagnose this rare sickness.

Doctor Shekhar was called as a consultant. When he heard the name of the city where she lived, a memory burned brightly in his eyes.

He got up and went to her room. As he entered her room, he immediately recognized her. He returned to the consultation room, determined to do his best to save her life.

From that day on, he paid special attention to this case. After a long battle, the war was finally won.

Doctor Shekhar left instructions that the bill should be sent to him for authorization. He looked it over, wrote something in the margin, and sent it to her room.

She thought that when she would open the envelope, she will find an invoice that would take the rest of her life to pay in full. But when she finally opened it, something caught her attention in the margin of the invoice.

Tears of joy filled her eyes and her heart when she read these words: paid in full with a glass of milk, signed Doctor Shekhar.

One evening an old monk told his grandson about a battle that goes on inside people. He said, "My son, the battle is between two "wolves" inside us all.

One is Evil. It is anger, envy, jealousy, sorrow, regret, greed, arrogance, self-pity, guilt, resentment, inferiority, lies, false pride, superiority and ego.

The other is Good. It is joy, peace, love, hope, serenity, humility, kindness, benevolence, empathy, generosity, truth, compassion and faith."

The grandson thought about it for a minute and then asked his grandfather: "Which wolf wins?"

The old monk simply replied, "the one you feed."

Put the Glass Down Today!

Professor began his class by holding up a glass with some water in it. He held it up for all to see and asked the students "How much do you think this glass weighs?"

'50 gms!' .... '100 gms!' .... '125 gms', the students answered.

"I really don't know unless I weigh it," said the professor, "but, my question is, what would happen if I held it up like this for a few minutes?"

"Nothing," the students said.

"Ok what would happen if I held it up like this for an hour?" the professor asked.

"Your arm would begin to ache," said one of the student.

"You're right, now what would happen if I held it for a day?"

"Your arm could go numb, you might have severe muscle stress and paralysis and have to go to hospital for sure!" ventured another student and all the students laughed.

"Very good. But during all this, did the weight of the glass change?" asked the professor.

"No." The students answered.

"Then what caused the arm ache and the muscle stress?"

The students were puzzled.

"What should I do now to come out of pain?" asked the professor again.

"Put the glass down!" said one of the students.

"Exactly!" said the professor.

Life's problems are something like this. Hold it for a few minutes in your head and they seem OK. Think of them for a long time and they begin to ache. Hold it even longer and they begin to paralyze you. You will not be able to do anything.

It's important to think of the challenges or problems in your life, but even more important is to 'PUT THEM DOWN' at the end of every day before you go to sleep.

That way, you are not stressed, you wake up every day fresh and strong and can handle any issue, any challenge that comes your way!

So, When you leave office today,

Remember friend to

'PUT THE GLASS DOWN!'

Life laughs at you when you are unhappy...

Life smiles at you when you are happy...

Life salutes you when you make others happy...

This too will Pass

Once a king called upon all of his wise men and asked them, "Is there a *mantra* or suggestion which works in every situation, in every circumstance, in every place and every time. Something which can help me when none of you is available to advise me." All wise men got puzzled by king's question. One answer for all questions. Something that works everywhere, in every situation. In every joy, every sorrow, every defeat and every victory. They thought and thought.

After a lengthy discussion, an old man suggested something which appealed to all of them. They went to the king and gave him something written on a paper. But the condition was that the king was not to see it out of curiosity. Only in extreme danger, when the king finds himself alone and there seems to be no way, only then he'll have to see it. The king put the paper under his diamond ring.

After a few days, the neighbors attacked the kingdom. It was a collective surprise attack of the king's enemies. King and his army fought bravely but lost the battle. King had to fled on his horse. The enemies were following him. His horse took him far away in the jungle. He could hear many troops of horses following him and the noise was coming closer and closer. Suddenly the king found himself standing at the end of the road. That road was not going anywhere. Underneath there was a rocky valley thousands of feet deep. If he jumped into it, he would be finished. The sound of enemy's horses was approaching fast. The king became restless. There seemed to be no way.

Then suddenly he saw the diamond in his ring shining in the sun, and he remembered the message hidden in the ring.

He read the message. The message was very small but very great. The message was—"This too will pass."

The king read it. Again read it. Suddenly something struck him—yes! this too will pass. Only a few days ago, I was enjoying my kingdom. I was the mightiest of all the kings. Yet today, the kingdom and all its pleasures have gone. I am here trying to escape from enemies. However when those days of luxuries have gone, this day of danger too will pass.

The revelation of the message had a great effect on him. Calm came on his face. He relaxed and forgot about those following him. After a few minutes he realized that the noise of the horses and the approaching enemy was receding. They had moved into some other part of the mountains and were not on that path anymore.

The king reorganized his army and fought again. He defeated the enemy and regained his lost empire. When he returned to his empire after victory, he was received with much funfare. The whole capital was rejoicing in the victory. Everyone was in a festive mood. Flowers were being thrown on the king from every house, from every corner.

People were dancing and singing. For a moment king said to himself, "I am one of the bravest and greatest kings. It is not easy to defeat me." With all the reception and celebration he saw an ego emerging in him.

Suddenly the diamond of his ring flashed in the sunlight and reminded him of the message. He opened it and read it again: "This too will pass." He became silent. His face went through a total change—from the egoist he moved to a state of utter humbleness.

Love and Life

My husband is engineer by profession. I love him for his steady nature and I love the warm feeling when I lean against his broad shoulders.

Two years of courtship and now, five years into marriage, I would have to admit, that I am getting tired of it. I am a sentimental woman and extremely sensitive when it comes to a relationship and my feelings. I yearn for the romantic moments, like a little girl yearning for candy. My husband is my complete opposite; his lack of sensitivity, and the inability of bringing romantic moments into our marriage has disheartened me about love.

One day, I finally decided to tell him my decision, that I wanted a divorce.

"Why?" he asked, shocked.

"I am tired. There are no reasons for everything in the world!" I answered.

He kept silent the whole night, seemingly in deep thought. My feeling of disappointment only increased. Here was a man who was not able to even express his predicament, so what else could I expect from him.

Finally he asked me: "What can I do to change your mind?"

Looking deep into his eyes I slowly answered: "Here is the question. If you can answer and convince my heart, I will change my mind. Let's say, I want a flower located on the face of a mountain cliff, and we both are sure that picking the flower will cause your death. Will you do it for me?"

He said: "I will give you your answer tomorrow...." My hopes just sank by listening to his response.

I woke up the next morning to find him gone, and saw a piece of paper with his scratchy handwriting underneath a milk glass, on the dining table near the front door, that goes....

"My dear, I would not pick that flower for you, but, please allow me to explain the reasons further." This first line was already breaking my heart. I continued reading.

"When you use the computer you always mess up the Software programs, and you cry in front of the screen. I have to save my fingers so that I can help to restore the programs.

You always leave the house keys behind, thus I have to save my legs to rush home to open the door for you.

You love traveling but always lose your way in a new city. I have to save my eyes to show you the way.

You like to stay indoors, and I have to save my mouth to tell you jokes and stories to cure your boredom.

You always stare at the computer, and that will do nothing good for your eyes. I have to save my eyes so that when we grow old, I can help to clip your nails and help to remove those annoying white hair. So I can also hold your hand while strolling down the beach, as you enjoy the sunshine and the beautiful sand.... and tell you the colour of flowers, just like the colour of the glow on your young face.

Thus, my dear, unless I am sure that there is someone who loves you more than I do... I could not pick that flower yet, and die ..."

My tears fell on the letter, and blurred the ink of his handwriting. I continued reading, "Now, that you have finished reading my answer, and if you are satisfied, please open the front door for I am standing outside bringing your favorite bread and fresh milk."

I rushed to pull open the door, and saw his anxious face, clutching tightly with his hands, the milk bottle and loaf of bread. Now I am very sure that no one will ever love me as much as he does, and I have decided to leave the flower alone.

Flowers, and romantic moments are only used and appear on the surface of the relationship. Under all this, the pillar of true love stands.

Food is important—but even more important is your mental and emotional diet. Keep it filled with the vitamins of love, faith, joy and forgiveness.

* * *

For every minute you are angry

You lose sixty seconds of happiness.

* * *

Don't tell God how big your problems are...

Tell your problems how big your God is!

Building a Life

An elderly carpenter was ready to retire, and he told his boss of his plans to leave and live a more leisurely life with his wife. He would miss the paycheck, but he needed to retire.

The contractor was sorry to see such a good worker go, and he asked the carpenter to build just one more house as a personal favor.

The carpenter said yes, but his heart was not in his work. He resorted to shoddy workmanship and used inferior material. It was an unfortunate way to end a dedicated career.

When the carpenter finished his work, the employer came to inspect the house. He handed the front-door key to the carpenter. "This is your house," he said. "It is my gift to you."

The carpenter was shocked! What a shame! If he had only known he was building his own house, he would have done it all so differently.

So it is with us. We build our lives, a day at a time, often putting less than our best into the building. Then with a shock we realize we have to live in the house we have built.

If we could do it over, we'd do it much differently. But we cannot go back.

You are the carpenter of your life. Each day you hammer a nail, place a board, or erect a wall.

Your attitudes and the choices you make today build your "house" for tomorrow...

Build wisely!

God's Clinic

I went to God's Clinic to have my routine check-up.

- When God took my blood pressure, He saw I was low in tenderness.
- When he read my temperature, the thermometer registered 40° of anxiety.
- He ran an electrocardiogram and found that I needed several 'love bypasses' since my arteries were blocked with loneliness and could not provide for an empty heart.
- I was advised to consult orthopedics, because I could not walk by my brother's side and I could not hug my friends, since I had fractured myself when tripping with envy.
- He also found I was shortsighted, since I could not see beyond the shortcomings of my brothers and sisters.
- When I complained about deafness, the diagnosis was that I had stopped listening to God's voice talking to me on a daily basis.

For all of that, God gave me a free consultation, thanks to his mercifulness. So my pledge is to, once I leave this clinic, only take the natural remedies he prescribed through his words of truth:

- Every morning, take a full glass of gratitude.
- When getting to work, take one spoon of peace.
- Every hour, take one pill of patience, one cup of brotherhood and one glass of humility.
- When getting home, take one dose of love.
- When getting to bed, take two tablets of clear conscience.

Thanks God, I have already started feeling better.

Have Faith

An atheist professor of philosophy speaks to his class on the problem science has with God, the Almighty. He asks one of his new students .....

Prof: You believe in God?

Student: Absolutely, sir.

Prof: Is God good?

Student: Sure.

Prof: Is God all-powerful?

Student: Yes.

Prof: My brother died of cancer even though he prayed to God to heal him. Most of us would attempt to help others who are ill. But God didn't. How is this God good then? Hmm?

(*Student is silent.*)

Prof: You can't answer, can you? Let's start again, young fellow. Is God good?

Student: Yes.

Prof: Is Satan good?

Student: No.

Prof: Where does Satan come from?

Student: From... God....

Prof: That's right. Tell me son, is there evil in this world?

Student: Yes.

Prof: Evil is everywhere, isn't it? And God did make everything. Correct?

Student: Yes.

Prof: So who created evil?

(*Student does not answer.*)

Prof: Is there sickness? Immorality? Hatred? Ugliness? All these terrible things exist in the world, don't they?

Student: Yes sir.

Prof: So who created them?

(*Student has no answer.*)

Prof: Science says you have 5 senses you use to identify and observe the world around you. Tell me, son... Have you ever seen God?

Student: No sir.

Prof: Tell us if you have ever heard your God?

Student: No sir.

Prof: Have you ever felt your God, tasted your God, smelt your God? Have you ever had any sensory perception of God for that matter?

Student: No sir. I'm afraid I haven't.

Prof: Yet you still believe in Him?

Student: Yes.

Prof: According to testable, demonstrable protocol, science says your God doesn't exist. What do you say to that, son?

Student: Nothing. I only have my faith.

Prof: Yes. Faith. And that is the problem science has.

Student: Professor, is there such a thing as heat?

Prof: Yes.

Student: And is there such a thing as cold?

Prof: Yes.

Student: No sir. There isn't.

(*The lecture theatre becomes very quiet with this turn of events.*)

Student: Sir, you can have lots of heat, even more heat, mega heat, superheat, a little heat or no heat. But we don't have anything called cold. We can hit 458 degrees below zero which is no heat, but we can't go any further after that. There is no such thing as cold. Cold is only a word we use to describe the absence of heat. We cannot measure cold. Heat is energy. Cold is not the opposite of heat, sir, just the absence of it.

(*There is pin-drop silence in the lecture theatre.*)

Student: What about darkness, Professor? Is there such a thing as darkness?

Prof: Yes. What is night if there isn't darkness?

Student: You're wrong again, sir. Darkness is the absence of something. You can have low light, normal light, bright light, flashing light..... But if you have no light constantly, you have nothing and it's called darkness, isn't it? In reality, darkness isn't. If it were, you would be able to make darkness darker, wouldn't you?

Prof: So what is the point you are making, young man?

Student: Sir, my point is your philosophical premise is flawed.

Prof: Flawed? Can you explain how?

Student: Sir, you are working on the premise of duality. You argue there is life and then there is death, a good God and a bad God. You are viewing the concept of God as something finite, something we can measure. Sir, science can't even explain a thought. It uses electricity and magnetism, but has never seen, much less fully understood either one.

To view death as the opposite of life is to be ignorant of the fact that death cannot exist as a substantive thing. Death is not the opposite of life, just the absence of it.

Now tell me, Professor. Do you teach your students that they evolved from a monkey?

Prof: If you are referring to the natural evolutionary process, yes, of course, I do.

Student: Have you ever observed evolution with your own eyes, sir?

(*The Professor shakes his head with a smile, beginning to realize where the argument is going.*)

Student: Since no one has ever observed the process of evolution at work and cannot even prove that this process is an on-going endeavour, are you not teaching your opinion, sir? Are you not a scientist but a preacher?

(*The class is in uproar.*)

Student: Is there anyone in the class who has ever seen the Professor's brain?

(*The class breaks out into laughter.*)

Student: Is there anyone here who has ever heard the Professor's brain, felt it, touched or smelt it? No one appears to have done so. So, according to the established rules of stable, demonstrable protocol, science says that you have no brain, sir. With all due respect, sir, how do we then trust your lectures, sir?

(*The room is silent. The professor stares at the student, his face unfathomable.*)

Prof: I guess you'll have to take them on faith, son.

Student: That is it sir. The link between man and God is faith. That is all that keeps things moving and alive.

God is not present in idols. Your feelings are your God. The soul is your temple.

I Wish you Enough

Recently I overheard a father and daughter in their last moments together at the airport. They had announced the departure. Standing near the security gate, they hugged and the father said, "I love you, and I wish you enough." The daughter replied, "Dad, our life together has been more than enough. Your love is all I ever needed. I wish you enough, too, Dad." They kissed and the daughter left.

The father walked over to the window where I was seated. Standing there I could see he wanted and needed to cry. I tried not to intrude on his privacy, but he welcomed me in by asking, "Did you ever say good-bye to someone knowing it would be forever?"

"Yes, I have," I replied. "Forgive me for asking, but why is this a forever good-bye?"

"I am old, and she lives so far away. I have challenges ahead and the reality is, the next trip back will be for my funeral," he said.

"When you were saying good-bye, I heard you say, 'I wish you enough.' May I ask what that means?"

He began to smile. "That's a wish that has been handed down from our generations. My parents used to say it to everyone." He paused a moment and looked up as if trying to remember it in detail, and he smiled even more.

"When we said, 'I wish you enough,' we were wanting the other person to have a life filled with just enough good things to sustain them."

Then turning toward me, he shared the following as if he was reciting it from memory.

- I wish you enough sun to keep your attitude bright no matter how grey the day may appear.

- I wish you enough rain to appreciate the sun even more.

- I wish you enough happiness to keep your spirit alive and everlasting.

- I wish you enough pain so that even the smallest of joys in life may appear bigger.

- I wish you enough gain to satisfy your wanting.

- I wish you enough loss to appreciate all that you possess.

- I wish you enough hellos to get you through the final good-bye.

If One Day...

If one day you feel like crying, call me. I don't promise that I will make you laugh, but I can cry with you.

If one day you don't want to listen to anyone, call me. I promise to be there for you. And I promise to be very quiet.

But if one day you call, and there is no answer; come fast to see me. Maybe I need you.

A Different Perspective

A blind boy sat on the steps of a building with a hat by his feet. He held up a sign which said: 'I am blind, please help.' There were only a few coins in the hat.

A man was walking by. He took a few coins from his pocket and dropped them into the hat. He then took the sign, turned it around, and wrote some words. He put the sign back so that everyone who walked by would see the new words.

Soon the hat began to fill up. A lot more people were giving money to the blind boy. That afternoon the man who had changed the sign came to see how things were.

The boy recognized his footsteps and asked, "Were you the one who changed my sign this morning? What did you write?"

The man said, "I only wrote the truth. I said what you said but in a different way."

What he had written was: 'Today is a beautiful day and I cannot see it.'

If you have an apple and I have an apple and we exchange these apples then you and I will still each have one apple. But if you have an idea and I have an idea and we exchange these ideas, then each of us will have two ideas.

Something for God to Do

This is God. Today I will be handling all of your problems for you. I do not need your help. So, have a nice day. I love you.

And remember, if life happens to deliver a situation to you that you cannot handle, do not attempt to resolve it yourself! Kindly put it in the SFGTD (Something For God To Do) box. I will get to it in My time. All situations will be resolved, but in My time, not yours.

Once the matter is placed into the box, do not hold onto it by worrying about it. Instead, focus on all the wonderful things that are present in your life now.

If you find yourself stuck in traffic, don't despair. There are people in this world for whom driving is an unheard of privilege.

Should you have a bad day at work; think of the man who has been out of work for years.

Should you despair over a relationship gone bad; think of the person who has never known what it's like to love and be loved in return.

Should you grieve the passing of another weekend; think of the woman in dire straits, working twelve hours a day, seven days a week to feed her children.

Should your car break down, leaving you miles away from assistance; think of the physically disabled, who would love the opportunity to take that walk.

Should you notice a new grey hair in the mirror; think of the cancer patient in chemo who wishes she had hair to examine.

Should you find yourself at a loss and pondering what is life all about, asking what is my purpose, be thankful. There are those who didn't live long enough to get the opportunity.

Should you find yourself the victim of other people's bitterness, ignorance, smallness or insecurities; remember, things could be worse. You could be one of them!

Now, you have a nice day.

God

No one will manufacture a lock without a key.
Similarly God won't give problems without solutions.

* * *

In a day, when you don't come across any problems—you can be sure that you are traveling in a wrong path.

* * *

Don't hurry, don't worry. You're here only for a short while. So be sure to stop and smell the flowers.

Priya and Her Mother-in-Law

A girl named Priya got married and went to live with her husband and mother-in-law. In a very short time, Priya found that she couldn't get along with her mother-in-law at all. Their personalities were very different, and Priya was angered by many of her mother-in-law's habits.

Days passed, and weeks passed. Priya and her mother-in-law never stopped arguing and fighting. All the anger and unhappiness in the house was causing Priya's poor husband great distress. Finally, Priya could not stand her mother-in-law any longer, and she decided to do something about it. She went to see her father's good friend, Prem, who sold herbs. She told him the situation and asked if he would give her some poison so that she could solve the problem for once and all.

Prem thought for a while, and finally said, "Priya, I will help you solve your problem, but you must listen to me and obey what I tell you." Priya said, "Yes, uncle, I will do whatever you tell me to do." Prem went into the back room, and returned in a few minutes with a package of herbs. He told Priya, "You can't use a quick-acting poison to get rid of your mother-in-law, because that would cause people to become suspicious. Therefore, I have given you a number of herbs that will slowly build up poison in her body. Every other day prepare some delicious meal and put a little of these herbs in her serving. Now, in order to make sure that nobody suspects you when she dies, you must be very careful to be actively friendly to her. Don't argue with her, obey her every wish, and treat her like a queen." Priya was so happy. She thanked Prem and hurried home to start her plot of murdering her mother-in-law.

93

Weeks went by, and months went by, and every other day, Priya served the specially treated food to her mother-in-law. She remembered what Prem had said about avoiding suspicion, so she controlled her temper, and treated her mother-in-law like her own mother.

After six months had passed, the whole household had changed. Priya had practiced controlling her temper so much that she found that she almost never got mad or upset. She hadn't had an argument with her mother-in-law in last six months because she now seemed much kinder and easier to get along with.

The mother-in-law's attitude towards Priya also changed, and she began to love Priya like her own daughter. She kept telling friends and relatives that Priya was the best daughter-in-law one could ever find. Priya and her mother-in-law were now treating each other like a real mother and daughter.

One day, Priya went to see Prem and asked for his help again. She said, "Dear uncle, please help me to keep the poison from killing my mother-in-law. She's changed into such a nice woman, and I love her like my own mother. I do not want her to die because of the poison I gave her."

Prem smiled and nodded his head. "Priya, there's nothing to worry about. I never gave you any poison. The herbs I gave you were vitamins to improve her health. The only poison was in your mind and your attitude towards her, but that has been all washed away by the love which you gave to her."

> *It is easier to protect your feet with slippers than to cover the earth with carpet.*

The Pretty Lady

Once upon a time a big monk and a little monk were traveling together. They came to the bank of a river and found the bridge was damaged. They had to wade across the river. There was a pretty lady who was stuck at the damaged bridge and couldn't cross the river. The big monk offered to carry her across the river on his back. The lady accepted.

The little monk was shocked by the move of the big monk. 'How can big brother carry a lady when we are supposed to avoid all intimacy with females' thought the little monk. But he kept quiet. The big monk carried the lady across the river and the small monk followed unhappily. When they crossed the river, the big monk let the lady down and they parted ways with her.

All along the way for several miles, the little monk was very unhappy with the act of the big monk. He was making up all kinds of accusations about big monk in his head. This got him madder and madder. But he still kept quiet. And the big monk had no inclination to explain his situation. Finally, at a rest point many hours later, the little monk could not stand it any further. He burst out angrily at the big monk, "How can you claim yourself a devout monk, when you seize the first opportunity to touch a female, especially when she is very pretty. All your teachings to me make you a big hypocrite."

The big monk looked surprised and said, "I had put down the pretty lady at the river bank many hours ago, how come you are still carrying her along?"

Burnt Toast

When I was a little girl, my mom liked to make breakfast food for dinner every now and then. And I remember one night in particular when she had made dinner after a long, hard day at work. On that evening so long ago, my mom placed a plate of eggs, milk, and extremely burned toast in front of my dad. I remember waiting to see if anyone noticed! Yet all my dad did was reach for his toast, smile at my mom, and ask me how my day was at school. I don't remember what I told him that night, but I do remember watching him smear butter and jelly on that toast and eat every bite! When I got up from the table that evening, I remember hearing my mom apologize to my dad for burning the toast. And I'll never forget what he said: "Baby, I love burned toast."

Later that night, I went to kiss daddy good night and I asked him if he really liked his toast burned. He wrapped me in his arms and said, "Sonia, your momma put in a hard day at work today and she's real tired. And besides, a little burnt toast never hurt anyone! You know, life is full of imperfect things..... and imperfect people. I'm not the best housekeeper or cook. What I've learned over the years is that learning to accept each other's faults—and choosing to celebrate each other's differences—is one of the most important keys to creating a healthy, growing, and lasting relationship."

> *Don't put the key to your happiness in someone else's pocket but into your own.*

Heaven and Hell

A Holy man was having a conversation with the Lord one day and said, "Lord, I would like to know what Heaven and Hell are like."

The Lord led the holy man to two doors. He opened one of the doors and the holy man looked in. In the middle of the room was a large round table. In the middle of the table was a large pot of stew, which smelled delicious and made the holy man's mouth water. The people sitting around the table were thin and sickly. They appeared to be famished. They were holding spoons with very long handles that were strapped to their arms and each found it possible to reach into the pot of stew and take a spoonful. But because the handle was longer than their arms, they could not get the spoons back into their mouths.

The holy man shuddered at the sight of their misery and suffering.

The Lord said, "You have seen Hell."

They went to the next room and opened the door. It was exactly the same as the first one. There was the large round table with the large pot of stew which made the holy man's mouth water. The people were equipped with the same long-handled spoons, but here the people were well nourished and plump, laughing and talking.

The holy man said, "I don't understand."

"It is simple," said the Lord. "It requires but one skill. You see, they have learned to feed each other. As they can not put the spoon in their mouth, they are feeding each other."

Game of Potato

A kindergarten teacher decided to let her class play a game. The teacher told each child in the class to bring along a plastic bag containing a few potatoes. Each potato will be given a name of a person that the child hates, so the number of potatoes that a child will put in his/her plastic bag will depend on the number of people he/she hates.

So when the day came, every child brought some potatoes with the name of the people he/she hated. Some had 2 potatoes; some 3 while some up to 5 potatoes. The teacher then told the children to carry with them the potatoes in the plastic bag wherever they went (even to the toilet) for 1 week.

Days after days passed by, and the children started to complain due to the unpleasant smell let out by the rotten potatoes. Besides, those having more potatoes had to carry heavier bags. After one week, the children were relieved because the game had finally ended.

The teacher asked: "How did you feel while carrying the potatoes with you for one week?" The children let out their frustrations and started complaining of the trouble that they had to go through having to carry the heavy and smelly potatoes wherever they went.

Then the teacher told them the hidden meaning behind the game. The teacher said: "This is exactly the situation when you carry your hatred for somebody inside your heart. The stench of hatred will contaminate your heart and you will carry it with you wherever you go. If you cannot tolerate the smell of rotten potatoes for just one week, can you imagine what is it like to have the stench of hatred in your heart for your lifetime?"

One Bedroom Flat

As the dream of most parents, I had acquired a degree in Engineering and joined a company based in USA, the land of opportunity. When I arrived in the USA, it was as if a dream had come true.

Here at last I was in the place where I wanted to be. I decided I would be staying in this country for about five years, in which time I would have earned enough money to settle down in India.

My father was a government employee and after his retirement, the only asset he could acquire was a decent one bedroom flat. I wanted to do some thing more than him.

I started feeling homesick and lonely as the time passed. I used to call home and speak to my parents every week using cheap international phone cards. Two years passed, two years of burgers at McDonald's and pizzas and two years watching the foreign exchange rate getting better whenever the Rupee value went down.

Finally I decided to get married. I told my parents that I have only 10 days of holidays and everything must be done within these 10 days. I got my ticket booked in the cheapest flight. Was jubilant and was actually enjoying shopping for gifts for all my friends back home. After reaching home I spent one week going through all the photographs of girls and as the time was getting shorter I was forced to select one candidate.

I realised, that I would have to get married in 2–3 days, as I will not get anymore holidays. After the marriage, it was time to return to USA. After giving some money to my parents and telling the neighbours to look after them, we returned to USA.

My wife enjoyed this country for about two months and then she started feeling lonely. The frequency of calling India increased to twice in a week, sometimes 3 times a week. Our savings started dwindling.

After two more years we started to have kids. Two lovely kids, a boy and a girl, were gifted to us by the almighty. Every time I spoke to my parents, they asked me to come to India so that they can see their grandchildren.

Every year I decided to go to India, but part work, part monetary conditions prevented it. Years went by and visiting India was a distant dream. Then suddenly one day I got a message that my parents were seriously sick. I tried but I couldn't get any holidays and thus could not go to India. The next message I got was that my parents had passed away and as there was no one to do the last rights, the society members had done whatever they could. I was depressed. My parents had passed away without seeing their grand-children.

After couple of more years passed away, much to my children's dislike and my wife's joy we returned to India to settle down. I started to look for a suitable property, but to my dismay my savings were short and the property prices had gone up during all these years. I had to return to the USA.

My wife refused to come back with me and my children refused to stay in India. My two children and I returned to USA after promising my wife I would be back for good after two years.

Time passed by. My daughter decided to get married to an American and my son was happy living in USA. I wound-up every thing and returned to India. I had just enough money to buy a decent two bedroom flat in a well-developed locality.

Now I am 60 years old and the only time I go out of the flat is for the routine visit to the nearby temple. My faithful wife has also left me and gone to the holy abode.

Sometimes I wonder, was it worth all this?

My father, even after staying in India, had a house to his name and I too have the same, nothing more.

I lost my parents and children for just ONE EXTRA BEDROOM. I get occasional cards from my children asking I am alright. Well at least they remember me.

Now perhaps after I die it will be the neighbours again who will be performing my last rights. God bless them.

But the question still remains 'was all this worth it?'

I am still searching for an answer!!!

It takes considerable knowledge just to realise the extent of our own ignorance.

The Daffodil Principle

Several times my daughter had telephoned to say, "Mother, you must come to see the daffodils before they are over."

I wanted to go, but it was a long drive from Solan to Mashobra.

"I will come next Tuesday," I promised a little reluctantly on her third call.

Next Tuesday dawned cold and rainy. Still, I had promised, and reluctantly I drove there. When I finally walked into Jyoti's house I was welcomed by the joyful sounds of happy children. I delightedly hugged and greeted my grandchildren.

"Forget the daffodils, Jyoti! The road is invisible in these clouds and fog, and there is nothing in the world except you and these children that I want to see badly enough to drive another inch!"

"But first we're going to see the daffodils. It's just a few blocks," Jyoti said. "I'll drive. I'm used to this. You will never forgive yourself if you miss this experience."

After about twenty minutes, we turned onto a small gravel road and I saw a small church. On the far side of the church, I saw a hand lettered sign with an arrow that read, 'Daffodil Garden'. We got out of the car, each took a child's hand, and I followed Jyoti down the path. Then, as we turned a corner, I looked up and gasped. Before me lay the most glorious sight.

It looked as though someone had taken a great vat of gold and poured it over the mountain and its surrounding slopes.

The flowers were planted in majestic, swirling patterns, great ribbons and swaths of deep orange, creamy white, lemon yellow, salmon pink, and saffron and butter yellow. Each different coloured variety was planted in large groups so that it swirled and flowed like its own river with its own unique hue. There were five acres of flowers.

"Who did this?" I asked Jyoti. "Just one woman," Jyoti answered. "She lives on the property. That's her house." Jyoti pointed to a well-kept small house, modestly sitting in the midst of all that glory.

We walked up to the house. On the patio, we saw a poster. 'Answers to the questions I know you are asking', was the headline. The first answer was a simple one. '50,000 bulbs', it read. The second answer was, 'One at a time, by one woman. Two hands, two feet, and one brain.' The third answer was, 'Began in 1961'.

For me, that moment was a life-changing experience. I thought of this woman whom I had never met, who, almost fifty years ago, had begun, one bulb at a time, to bring her vision of beauty and joy to an obscure mountaintop. Planting one bulb at a time, year after year, this unknown woman had forever changed the world in which she lived. One day at a time, she had created something of extraordinary magnificence, beauty, and inspiration. The principle her daffodil garden taught is one of the greatest principles of celebration.

That is, learning to move toward our goals and desires one step at a time, often just one baby step at a time and learning to love the doing, learning to use the accumulation of time. When we multiply tiny pieces of time with small increments of daily effort, we too will find we can accomplish magnificent things. We can change the world.

"It makes me sad in a way," I admitted to Jyoti. "What might I have accomplished if I had thought of a wonderful goal thirty-five or forty years ago and had worked away at it 'one bulb at a time' through all those years? Just think what I might have been able to achieve!"

My daughter summed up the message of the day in her usual direct way. "Start tomorrow," she said.

She was right. It's so pointless to think of the lost hours of yesterdays. The way to make learning a lesson of celebration instead of a cause for regret is only to ask, "How can I put this to use today?"

A journey of a thousand miles starts with a single step.

* * *

I long to accomplish a great and noble task, but it is my chief duty to accomplish small tasks as if they were great and noble.

* * *

If we did all the things we are capable of doing, we would literally astonish ourselves.

It is Easier to Criticize

Once upon a time there was a painter who had just completed his course under disciplehood of a great painter. This young artist decided to assess his skills. He gave his best strokes on the canvas. He took three days and painted a beautiful scenery.

He wanted people's opinion about his caliber and painting skills. So he put his creation at a busy street-crossing. He also put a board which read, "Gentlemen, I have painted this piece. Since I'm new to this profession, I might have committed some mistakes in my strokes etc. Please put a cross wherever you see a mistake."

When he came back in the evening to collect his painting he was completely shattered to see that the whole canvas was filled with Xs (crosses) and some people had even written their comments on the painting.

Disheartened and broken completely, he ran to his master's place and burst into tears. Sobbing and crying he told his master about what happened and showed the pathetic state of his creation which was filled with crosses and correction remarks.

The young artist was breathing heavily while the master heard him saying "I'm useless and if this is what I have learnt to paint I'm not worth becoming a painter. People have rejected me completely. I feel like dying."

Master smiled and suggested "My Son, I will prove that you are a great artist and have learnt to paint flawlessly."

Young disciple couldn't believe it and said, "I have lost faith in me and I don't think I am good enough. Don't make false hopes."

"Do as I say without questioning it. It will work." Master interrupted him.

Young artist reluctantly agreed and two days later early morning he presented a replica of his earlier painting to his master. Master took that gracefully and smiled. "Come with me," he said.

They reached the same street-square early morning and displayed the same painting exactly at the same place. Now master took out another board which read, "Gentlemen, I have painted this piece. Since I'm new to this profession, I might have committed some mistakes in my strokes etc. I have put a box with colors and brushes just below. Please do me a favor. If you see a mistake, kindly pick up the brush and correct it."

Master and disciple walked back home. They both visited the place same evening. Young painter was surprised to see that actually there was not a single correction done so far.

Next day again they visited and found the painting remained untouched. The painting was kept there for a month but no correction came in.

Moral: It is easier to criticize, but difficult to improve.

The glory is not in never failing, but in rising every time you fall.

A Dozen Questions to Ask Yourself

An old proverb says, "He that cannot ask cannot live." If you want answers you have to ask questions. These are 12 questions you should ask yourself and try to answer. You can ask yourself these questions right now and over the course of your life.

1. Am I doing what I really want to do?

2. What is my purpose?

3. What can I do to change the world?

4. What do I need to change about myself?

5. Do I take time out for myself and my family?

6. Do I listen to my heart?

7. Do I smile more than I frown?

8. Do I surround myself with good people?

9. Do I thank people enough?

10. What am I most proud of?

11. Do I help others?

12. Why not me?

> *No one can go back and change a bad beginning;*
>
> *But anyone can start new and create a successful ending.*

A Love Story of all Times

An incredible love story has come out of China recently and managed to touch the world. It is a story of a man and an older woman who ran off to live and love each other in peace for over half a century.

The 70-year-old Chinese man who hand-carved over 6,000 stairs up a mountain for his 80-year-old wife has passed away in the cave which has been the couple's home for the last 50 years.

Over 50 years ago, Liu Guojiang, a 19 year-old boy, fell in love with a 29 year-old widowed mother named Xu Chaoqin.

In a twist worthy of Shakespeare's Romeo and Juliet, friends and relatives criticized the relationship because of the age difference and the fact that Xu already had children.

At that time, it was unacceptable and immoral for a young man to love an older woman. To avoid the market gossip and the scorn of their communities, the couple decided to elope and lived in a cave in Jiangjin County in Southern Chong Qing Municipality.

In the beginning, life was harsh as they had nothing, no electricity or even food. They had to eat grass and roots they found in the mountain, and Liu made a kerosene lamp that they used to light up their lives.

Xu felt that she had tied Liu down and repeatedly asked him, "Are you regretful?" Liu always replied, "As long as we are industrious, life will improve."

In the second year of living in the mountain, Liu began and continued for over 50 years, to hand-carve the steps so that his wife could get down the mountain easily.

Half a century later in 2001, a group of adventurers were exploring the forest and were surprised to find the elderly couple and the over 6,000 hand-carved steps. Liu Ming Sheng, one of their seven children said, "My parents loved each other so much, they have lived in seclusion for over 50 years and never been apart a single day. He hand carved more than 6,000 steps over the years for my mother's convenience, although she doesn't go down the mountain that much."

The couple had lived in peace for over 50 years. Liu, when he was 72 years, returned from his daily farm work and collapsed. Xu sat and prayed for her husband as he passed away in her arms. So much in love with Xu, was Liu, that no one was able to release the grip he had on his wife's hand even after he had passed away.

"You promised me you'll take care of me, you'll always be with me until the day I died. Now you have left before me, how am I going to live without you?" Xu spent days softly repeating this sentence and touching her husband's black coffin with tears rolling down her cheeks.

In 2006, their story became one of the top 10 love stories from China, collected by the Chinese Women Weekly. The local government has decided to preserve the love ladder and the place they lived as a museum, so this love story can live forever.

As You Sow, so shall You Reap

"Good morning!" said a woman as she walked up to the man sitting on ground.

The man slowly looked up. This was a woman clearly accustomed to the finer things of life. Her coat was new. She looked like she had never missed a meal in her life. His first thought was that she wanted to make fun of him, like so many others had done before.

"Leave me alone," he growled. To his amazement, the woman continued standing. She was smiling—her even white teeth displayed in dazzling rows.

"Are you hungry?" she asked.

"No," he answered sarcastically. "I've just come from dining with the president. Now go away."

The woman's smile became even broader.

Suddenly the man felt a gentle hand under his arm. "What are you doing, lady?" the man asked angrily. "I said to leave me alone."

Just then a policeman came up. "Is there any problem, ma'am?" he asked.

"No problem here, officer," the woman answered. "I'm just trying to get this man on his feet. Will you help me?"

The officer scratched his head. "That's old Jack. He's been a fixture around here for a couple of years. What do you want from him?"

"See that cafeteria over there?" she asked. "I'm going to get him something to eat and get him out of the cold for a while."

"Are you crazy, lady?" the homeless man resisted. "I don't want to go in there!" Then he felt strong hands grab his other arm and lift him up.

"Let me go, officer. I didn't do anything."

"This is a good deal for you, Jack," the officer answered. "Don't blow it."

Finally, and with some difficulty, the woman and the police officer got Jack into the cafeteria and sat him at a table in a remote corner. It was the middle of the morning, so most of the breakfast crowd had already left and the lunch bunch had not yet arrived.

The manager strode across the cafeteria and stood by his table. "What's going on here, officer?" he asked. "What is all this, is this man in trouble?"

"This lady brought this man in here to be fed," the policeman answered.

"Not in here!" the manager replied angrily. "Having a person like that here is bad for business."

Old Jack smiled a toothless grin. "See, lady. I told you so. Now if you'll let me go. I didn't want to come here in the first place."

The woman turned to the cafeteria manager and smiled. "Sir, are you familiar with Eddy and Associates, the banking firm down the street?"

"Of course I am," the manager answered impatiently. "They hold their weekly meetings in one of my banquet rooms."

"And do you make a goodly amount of money providing food at these weekly meetings?"

"What business is that of yours?"

I, sir, am Penelope Eddy, president and CEO of the company."

"Oh....."

The woman smiled again. "I thought that might make a difference."

She glanced at the cop who was busy stifling a laugh. "Would you like to join us in a cup of coffee and a meal, officer?"

"No thanks, ma'am," the officer replied. "I'm on duty."

"Then, perhaps, a cup of coffee to go?"

"Yes, ma'am. That would be very nice."

The cafeteria manager turned on his heel. "I'll get your coffee for you right away, officer."

The officer watched him walk away. "You certainly put him in his place," he said.

"That was not my intent... Believe it or not, I have a reason for all this."

She sat down at the table across from her amazed dinner guest. She stared at him intently.

"Jack, do you remember me?"

Old Jack searched her face with his old, rheumy eyes. "I think so—I mean you do look familiar."

"I'm a little older perhaps," she said. "Maybe I've even filled out more than in my younger days when you worked here, and I came through that very door, cold and hungry."

"Ma'am?" the officer said questioningly. He couldn't believe that such a magnificently turned out woman could ever have been hungry.

"I was just out of college," the woman began. "I had come to the city looking for a job, but I couldn't find anything. Finally I was down to my last few cents and had been kicked out of my apartment. I walked the streets for days. It was February and I was cold and nearly starving. I saw this place and walked in to take a chance so that I could get something to eat."

Jack lit up with a smile. "Now I remember," he said. "I was behind the serving counter. You came up and asked me if you could work for something to eat. I said that it was against company policy."

"I know," the woman continued. "Then you made me the biggest roast beef sandwich that I had ever seen, gave me a cup of coffee, and told me to go over to a corner table and enjoy it. I was afraid that you would get into trouble. Then, when I looked over and saw you put the price of my food in the cash register, I knew then that everything would be all right."

"So you started your own business?" Old Jack asked.

"I got a job that very afternoon. I worked my way up. Eventually I started my own business, that, with the help of God, prospered." She opened her purse and pulled out a business card. "When you are finished here, I want you to pay a visit to a Mr. Lyons. He's the personnel director of my company. I'll go talk to him now and I'm certain he'll find something for you to do around the office."

She smiled. "I think he might even find the funds to give you a little advance so that you can buy some clothes and get a place to live until you get on your feet. If you ever need anything, my door is always open to you."

There were tears in the old man's eyes. "How can I ever thank you?" he asked.

"Don't thank me," the woman answered. "To God goes the glory. He led me to you."

Outside the cafeteria, the officer and the woman paused at the entrance before going their separate ways. "Thank you for all your help, officer," she said.

"On the contrary, Ms. Eddy," he answered. "Thank you. I saw a miracle today, something that I will never forget. And thank you for the coffee."

The quickest way to lift our living level is to lift our giving level.

* * *

Do you know, why God created gaps between fingers?

So that someone who is special to you, comes and fills those gaps by holding your hands.

* * *

A candle loses nothing if it is used to light another one.

Make Room

Think ....

Have you got the habit of hoarding useless objects, thinking that one day, who knows when, you may need them.

Have you got the habit of accumulating money, and not spending it because you think that in the future you may be in want of it.

Have you got the habit of storing clothes, shoes, furniture, utensils and other home supplies that you haven't used already for some time.

And inside yourself, have you got the habit to keep reproaches, resentment, sadness, fear and more.

Don't do it! You are going against your prosperity!

As long as you are, materially or emotionally, holding old and useless feelings, you won't have room for new opportunities.

Goods must circulate....

Clean your drawers, the wardrobes, the workshop, the garage...

Give away what you don't use any longer.

Get rid of what lost its colour and brightness.

Let the new enter your home.

May prosperity and peace reach you soon.

Amén!

The Missing Watch

Once there was a farmer who discovered that he had lost his watch in the barn. It was no ordinary watch because it had sentimental value for him. After searching high and low among the hay for a long while, he gave up and sought the help of a group of children playing outside the barn. He promised them that the person who found it would be rewarded.

Hearing this, the children hurried inside the barn, went through and around the entire stack of hay but still could not find the watch. Just when the farmer was about to give up looking for his watch, a little boy went up to him and asked to be given another chance.

The farmer looked at him and thought, "Why not? After all, this kid looks sincere enough."

So the farmer sent the little boy back in the barn. After a while the little boy came out with the watch in his hand! The farmer was both happy and surprised and so he asked the boy how he succeeded where the rest had failed.

The boy replied, "I did nothing but sit on the ground and listen. In the silence, I heard the ticking of the watch and just looked for it in that direction."

You never really lose until you quit trying.

* * *

Change your thoughts and you change your world.

Lessons of Life

I feared being alone,
until I learned to like myself.

I feared failure,
until I realized that I only fail when I don't try.

I feared rejection,
until I learned to have faith in myself.

I feared pain,
until I learned that it's necessary for growth.

I feared life and love
until I experienced its beauty.

I feared my destiny,
until I realized that I had the power to change my life.

I feared ridicule,
until I learned how to laugh at myself.

I feared growing old,
until I realized that I gained wisdom every day.

I feared the past,
until I realized that it could no longer hurt me.

I feared darkness,
until I saw the beauty of the starlight.

I feared change,
until I saw that even the most beautiful butterfly had to
undergo a metamorphosis before it could fly.

Deposit

Imagine that you had won the following prize in a contest:

Each morning your bank would deposit ₹ 86,400.00 in your account for your use. However, this prize has rules. The set of rules would be:

1. Everything that you didn't spend during each day would be taken away from you.
2. You may not simply transfer money into some other account.
3. You may only spend it.
4. Each morning upon awakening, the bank opens your account with another ₹ 86,400.00 for that day.
5. The bank can end the game without warning; at any time it can say, 'it's over', the game is over! It can close the account and you will not receive a new one.

What would you personally do?

You would buy anything and everything you wanted, right? Not only for yourself, but for all the people you love, even for people you don't know, because you couldn't possibly spend it all on yourself. You would try to spend every rupee, and use it all, right?

Well, each of us is in possession of such a magical bank. We just can't seem to see it. The magical bank is TIME!

1. Each morning we awaken to receive 86,400 seconds as a gift of life.
2. When we go to sleep at night, any remaining time is not credited to us.

3. What we haven't lived up that day is lost forever.

4. Each morning the account is refilled, but the bank can dissolve your account at any time without warning.

What will you do with your 86,400 seconds? These seconds are worth so much more than the same amount in rupees.

So, enjoy every second of your life. Take care of yourself, be happy, love deeply and enjoy life. Start spending!

With gratitude for the past and a blessing for the future, concentrate on living in the eternal now.

✳ ✳ ✳

Just 3 keys to enjoy life:

CTRL + ALT + DEL

*1. **Control** yourself*

*2. Look for **Alternative** solutions.*

*3. **Delete** the situation which gives you tension.*

✳ ✳ ✳

"Changing the Face" can change nothing.

But "Facing the Change" can change everything.

A Lizard Story

In order to renovate the house, someone in Japan broke open the wall. Japanese houses normally have a hollow space between the wooden walls. When tearing down the walls, he found that there was a lizard stuck there because a nail from outside had hammered into one of its feet.

He saw this and felt pity, and at the same time curious, as when he checked the nail, it was nailed 10 years ago, when the house was first built.

What happened?

The lizard had survived in such a position for 10 years! In a dark wall partition for 10 years without moving. It is impossible and mind-boggling.

Then he wondered how this lizard survived for 10 years without moving a single step, since its foot was nailed.

So he stopped his work and observed the lizard, what it had been doing, and what and how it had been eating.

Later, not knowing from where it came, appeared another lizard, with food in its mouth.

Ah! He was stunned and touched deeply.

For the lizard that was stuck by nail, another lizard had been feeding it for the past 10 years...

Imagine! it had been doing that untiringly for 10 long years, without giving up hope on its partner.

Would you do that for your partner?